T0243472

THE

SAILOR'S
BOOKSHELF

THE
SAILOR'S
BOOKSHELF

FIFTY BOOKS TO KNOW THE SEA
ADM. JAMES STAVRIDIS, USN (RET.)

 NAVAL INSTITUTE PRESS
ANNAPOLIS, MARYLAND

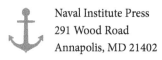

Naval Institute Press
291 Wood Road
Annapolis, MD 21402

Library of Congress Cataloging-in-Publication Data
Names: Stavridis, James, author.
Title: The sailor's bookshelf : fifty books to know the sea / Adm. James G.
  Stavridis, USN (Ret.).
Description: Annapolis, Maryland : Naval Institute Press, [2021] | Includes
  bibliographical references.
Identifiers: LCCN 2021024714 (print) | LCCN 2021024715 (ebook) | ISBN
  9781682476987 (hardcover) | ISBN 9781682477168 (ebook) | ISBN
  9781682477168 (pdf)
Subjects: LCSH: Sea in literature. | Sailors in literature. | Sea
  stories—History and criticism
Classification: LCC PN56.S4 S73 2021 (print) | LCC PN56.S4 (ebook) | DDC
  809/.9332162—dc23
LC record available at https://lccn.loc.gov/2021024714
LC ebook record available at https://lccn.loc.gov/2021024715

29 28 27 26 25 24 23 22   9 8 7 6 5 4 3 2

To my parents who taught me to love reading,
To my teachers who taught me to love writing,
To my shipmates who taught me to love the sea, and
To my wife and daughters who taught me to love life.

CONTENTS

EXPLORERS

SAILORS IN FICTION

SAILORS IN NONFICTION

PREFACE

I must down to the seas again, to the lonely sea and the sky,
And all I ask is a tall ship and a star to steer her by;
And the wheel's kick and the wind's song and the white sail's shaking,
And a grey mist on the sea's face, and a grey dawn breaking.

—"Sea Fever" by John Masefield

I have had three great passions in my life.

The first and most important is my lovely wife, Laura, to whom this book is dedicated. I met Laura in Athens, Greece—after a long sea voyage to arrive there—in 1962, when I was eight years old and Laura was only three. While perhaps not literally love at first sight, over many years our relationship grew into the deepest of love stories. The arrival of two daughters and, at this writing, four grandchildren has only intensified my belief that love and marriage are at the center of my life. But it is the other two passions that are at the heart of this book.

The second passion is one of the twin subjects of this volume: reading. From my earliest days, I've loved the feeling of holding a book in my hand (or even, today, of opening my Kindle). As I do so, I imagine the voyage upon which I am about to embark. It may be a work of historical fiction that will transport me to another time and place. The book before me may be a memoir that allows me access to the inner thoughts and deepest views of a famous historical figure. I may be about to cross a magical threshold and find myself in an entirely imagined vision of the future of the planet. Or the book in my hand can be the launch of a journey to some heretofore unknown part of the earth.

All of this began in earnest in my boyhood in the early 1960s while I was living with my family in Athens. Because there was no television accessible to a small American boy, I never developed the habit of watching the cartoons, situation comedies, and adventure shows that most young boys loved in those days. Instead, my mother, Shirley, would take me every week to the small but well-stocked English-language library at the U.S. Embassy, and we'd check out a stack of books. We also ventured to English-language bookstores in Greece, went to the small military exchange on the military base, and ordered books by mail from the United States. Every year on my birthday and Christmas, my principal gift would be a box of books. I've always believed that reading allows an individual to essentially expand their life every time they open a book, and that sense began when I was very young and continues to this day.

The third passion in my life is the ocean. I first went to sea, and truly out of sight of land, in the summer of 1962 when my family embarked on the old cruise liner SS *Constitution* out of New York, bound for Athens. We stopped in Boston, then sailed across the Atlantic to Lisbon, Naples, and finally arrived in Athens. From the moment I felt the ship lurch under my feet, I had a sense that I was home. Since my father was a U.S. Marine combat infantry officer, I had at least some connection with the U.S. Navy, given the ties of the Marine Corps and its sister service, the Navy. Throughout the years we lived in Greece, where my father served at the embassy as the assistant naval attaché, the sea was everywhere. Greece is, of course, one of the ancient centers of seafaring, and our vacations in the country were always on the seacoast. We went often to the small village of Itea, located near what is today the Corinth Canal and serves as the coastal gateway to the famous shrine at Delphi.

Much later, after I gained entrance to the U.S. Naval Academy with the idea of following in my father's footsteps as a Marine infantry officer, I was sent to sea in the summer of 1972 as part of my training. After a midshipman completes his or her first year at the academy, they are typically assigned to a U.S. Navy warship for a two-month period of apprenticeship in the summer months. For me, that ship was USS *Jouett* (DLG 29), a beautiful and relatively new guided missile destroyer whose home port was San Diego. We arrived on the ship in late June, and almost immediately—after loading the midshipmen on board—set sail for Hawaii. It was a spectacular California summer evening, and as the sun began to sink into the calm Pacific waters, I reported to the bridge for my first watch under way. As I walked onto the bridge, I looked out on a red setting sun, beautiful light playing on the water, and felt the gentle rocking of the ship encountering the first swells of the open ocean as we cleared the San Diego channel outbound. I was like Saint Paul on the road to Damascus—I knew at that moment that I wanted to be a sailor.

So I became a surface warfare officer and over the next forty years proudly sailed the world's oceans as a naval officer. I have spent roughly a decade, day for day, on the deep ocean out of sight of land in the course of serving in destroyers, cruisers, and aircraft carriers over the years. My time in command at sea remains a true-life highlight, and—although I missed my wife and daughters terribly during the course of many deployments—I loved my life at sea. And one of the principal enjoyments for me across all of those years was reading, sometimes in a small stateroom as a junior officer; on a couch in the wardroom after an evening watch; seated on a folding deck chair on a quiet Sunday at sea; in the more expansive stateroom of a commanding officer; in the captain's chair on a bridge wing; and eventually in the grand quarters of a flag officer embarked in an aircraft carrier.

This book is the result of the woven fabric of my life at sea with my endless love of books. I hope that by sharing this collection of fifty books—a true sailor's bookshelf—I can introduce and communicate my passion for both the oceans and books. Today in my library at home in Florida, I have more than five thousand books. Laura, who knows well my affection for both books and the sea, would say it is a "gentle madness." And as I walk by the rows of history, memoir, geography, oceanography, navigation, shiphandling, and fiction, they really do call out to me. Picking only half-a-hundred was a hard, hard set of choices, and many of my fellow sailors will be sad to discover that a favorite of theirs is not on this list. But I've tried hard to find the right balance between fiction and nonfiction, between oceans of the world, and between periods of history. Likewise, I've included some of the most fundamental texts that help sailors learn and hone their craft.

Each book is introduced with a quote and a simple sentence or two as to why it was chosen. I've then briefly sketched out my own experience with the book, connecting it to my long life at sea. For each, I've tried to provide a concise snapshot of what the book contains and then concluded with a final thought to take away. For books as different as *Moby-Dick* and *Naval Shiphandler's Guide*, the common thread is simple: these are books about the sea, with wisdom within their covers that will help anyone—whether a sailor or not—deepen their understanding and appreciation for the blue world that covers 70 percent of this planet.

A love of the sea, and a true understanding of the oceans, cannot be learned simply by reading books. But first and foremost, my simple hope in this small volume is that I can introduce the maritime world, in all of its splendor and diversity, to readers who do not know it well. And I hope as well that seasoned sailors will find some new treasures on this list, perhaps refresh themselves on a classic they read many years ago, or even argue with me about a favorite work that does not appear in these pages or about my interpretation of one that does. It is a voyage well worth taking, and as you pick up this book, we shall become shipmates and take it together.

Let's get under way.

THE OCEANS

CHAPTER ONE

ATLANTIC
Great Sea Battles, Heroic Discoveries, Titanic Storms, and a Vast Ocean of a Million Stories

by Simon Winchester

The outline of the Atlantic Ocean that we know today was fixed perhaps ten million years ago, and though to us and our cartographers it appears to have retained its boundaries, its coastlines and its look ever since . . . it has been changing, subtly and slightly all the time.[1]

As I mentioned in the preface, the first time I crossed the Atlantic Ocean was in 1962, when I was seven years old when my family headed to Athens, Greece. The SS *Constitution* was hardly a "luxury liner" by today's cruising standards, but it was very comfortable for the times. Laid down in 1951, she sailed for American Export Line's "Sunlane" cruise for her first couple of decades of service, plying the New York City–Lisbon-Gibraltar-Naples route. She was not a big liner compared to today's behemoths but weighed in at a respectable 25,000 tons, at nearly 700 feet in length, and a nice wide beam of almost 90 feet. Her top speed was around twenty-three knots, and there were decent accommodations for about a thousand passengers. My mother was happy to know that Grace Kelly, Cary Grant, Deborah Kerr, and even President Harry S. Truman had sailed in the ship in the past. There were very nice photos of them in the dining room.

Every day there were plenty of "kid" activities on board the ship for an active seven-year-old, but all I really wanted to do was walk around the upper decks and get to know the sea. What fascinated me then, and still does so many decades later, was the unpredictability of the ocean. It could change color, smell, wave pattern, surface condition, and a dozen other variables in an hour. It was a chameleon, and even then—as a small boy—I sensed the inherent danger in the fickle and ultimately uncaring Atlantic Ocean. I've gone on to sail each of the world's oceans and many of the smaller seas all around the globe. I've come to know well the Pacific, Indian, Arctic, and Antarctic Oceans. But the least predictable, most dangerous, and certainly most historically interesting, in my view, is the Atlantic. As is the case with your first kiss, I guess you could say you never forget your first ocean, and mine was the Atlantic.

All of this was doubly reinforced by my having been born in south Florida, in West Palm Beach, on the edge of the Gulf Stream. Over the years I've sailed much of the Atlantic, often in the Gulf Stream or into the Caribbean, or passing out of the southern reaches both through the Cape of Good Hope and Cape Horn. I've sailed by or visited many of the islands that dot the central Atlantic, many of which were touchstones for the great voyages of exploration. And I've done more than my share of voyages through the north Atlantic, which has seen both death and destruction in world wars as well as ushered the greatest explorers from Europe to the new world. I've studied the history and sailed the Atlantic waters through much of my life, and today I live on the mid-Atlantic in a beach town near Jacksonville, Florida, at the northern border of our most coastal state. I see the Atlantic Ocean every day, and it continues to fascinate me as it did when I was a boy. Thus, I was thrilled when Simon Winchester wrote what is essentially an anecdotal biography of the Atlantic. His subtitle captures the book well: *Great Sea Battles, Heroic Discoveries, Titanic Storms, and a Vast Ocean of a Million Stories.*

Storytelling is what Simon Winchester excels at, and he has managed throughout his career to find fascinating characters and share their tales with the reader.

A British subject (with American citizenship as well), he had a long run at the *Guardian*, one of the leading newspapers of the United Kingdom, beginning in the late 1960s. He has covered major stories globally, including the fall of Richard Nixon while Winchester was serving as the Washington correspondent for the paper. He then moved on in the early 1980s to the *Sunday Times* and was assigned to the Falklands campaign, where he was held prisoner briefly by the Argentine military. Shifting to freelance writing, he wrote a string of very successful non-fiction books about events and people around the world. In 2010 he published *Atlantic* to strong critical and commercial success.

The book has a "Shakespearean" structure in that it looks at the ocean through the prism of the seven ages of man from the play *As You Like It*: infant, schoolboy, lover, soldier, justice, "slippered pantaloon," and childlike elder. While this may be excessively poetic for some, to me it evokes the changing nature of this ocean. Like James A. Michener does in his book *Hawaii* (and in most of his books set in various locales), Winchester begins with the geology and science of the foundation of the Atlantic. But, Winchester points out, even after discovering the Atlantic outside the pillars of Hercules (Gibraltar), many centuries pass—and the Cretans, Greeks, Phoenicians, Egyptians, and Romans essentially ignore it. Only the Vikings in very small numbers sail the north Atlantic, and there is not widespread exploration until roughly 1500 AD, after the 1492 voyage of Columbus. From the beginning of sailing the seas, most sailors feared the Atlantic. "There be dragons (or monsters) here" was often written on early charts over the waters past Gibraltar.

Eventually men decided to sail the Atlantic, and Winchester is at his best describing the age of exploration that follows, laying out the various competing European adventurers in bold strokes. He tells story after story, weaving them together into a compelling portrait of this vast body of water and those who sailed it for hundreds of years after Columbus. The vicious triangular slave trade is exposed in all its venality and horror. For a Navy officer, the sections of the book about the great sea battles of the Armada, Trafalgar, and the two world wars shine brightly. We also learn about the battle for fish, especially the storied cod. Winchester also touches on the ecology and environment, including the high percentage of global oxygen produced by photosynthesis in the sea. All of this is laid out for a body of water that covers 20 percent of the world's surface but holds a far higher percentage of its history. The Atlantic Ocean has been at the crossroads of history for well over half a millennium and will continue to be a bridge between the United States and our closest pool of partners and allies. By the time a sailor puts this book down, he or she will indeed know well this ocean and its impact on the past and present.

Bonus: Winchester went on to write another book about that mother of all oceans, the truly vast Pacific, in *Pacific: The Ocean of the Future* (London: Williams Collins, 2015).

CHAPTER TWO

ATLAS OF REMOTE ISLANDS
Fifty Islands I Have Never Set Foot On and Never Will

by Judith Schalansky

Paradise is an island. So is hell.[1]

More than 70 percent of the surface of the world is covered by the sea. And the vast majority of countries are part of the major land masses—the continents of North America, South America, Europe, Asia, Africa, Australia, and Antarctica. There are some *very* large islands, of course: Greenland, New Guinea, Borneo, Madagascar, Baffin, Sumatra, Honshu, Victoria, Great Britain, and Ellesmere are the top ten, depending on how you measure them—with little-known Baffin, Victoria, and Ellesmere part of the Canadian archipelago in the high north. But Judith Schalansky's fascinating little gem of a book is concerned with tiny, largely unknown islands scattered around the world. Schalansky essentially selected them largely for how far they are from big, continental lands. Even after spending a significant portion of my life at sea,

I can only claim to have visited or even sailed within sight of about a dozen of them. Most of these small atolls are far from their mother countries, and only even exist on a map in a little box slipped in at the side of the page, much like a "little kids' table" at Thanksgiving dinner.

But each of these isolated islands has a story that is inextricably tied to the sea. Throughout recorded history, mariners have departed the big continents and sailed into initially unknown waters. At times they discovered massive continents, of course; but in many, many instances, intrepid sailors and explorers found themselves turning a ship to port or starboard, following a lookout's cry of *Land ho!* upon sighting a small island. Eyes on deck would follow the pointing arm of a seaman clutching a swaying mast far above the surface of the sea. The intrepid explorers would then seek to sail around the island, wondering what was on that sometimes "fatal shore"? Gold and jewels? Heathens to be converted to the cross? Arable land and fresh water? What treasures await?

If the circumnavigation was promising, it would be followed by a landing party and a more detailed survey. Each of the fifty islands in Schalansky's book has a distinct story that typically starts at that moment of discovery—a moment that, sadly, frequently turned out badly for the indigenous people of the island, who were most often displaced by colonizing populations. Today, most of the islands now have mixed populations of very small numbers of people, clinging to a life that is far, far removed from what the vast majority of us experience in the day-to-day world. The sea surrounds them and is the immediate border of their visual lives. Do the people on these islands feel isolated? Of course, but on the other hand, it takes only a determined shift of perspective to believe that you exist in the "navel of the world," as the Rapa Nui of Easter Island consider themselves. Is it heaven or hell to find yourself in a tiny place, far from civilization, whatever that means in today's world?

Schalansky has created a beautifully curated tour of the ocean world by sharing a small but accurate map of each island, adding signposts of the distances to the major ports (which are, in all cases, very far away) and sketching the history of each island in tight, vivid essays. As she says, "it is high time for cartography to take its place among the arts."[2] Each of the little stories in this slim volume illuminates a slice of the earth that few other than deep-sea mariners will know. For those of us who have called at one of these islands, or sailed within sight, this book is a reminder of the vast distances of the oceans. Indeed, I once sailed more than a week across the deep Pacific without sight of land, or of another ship, and with not even another vessel appearing on our radar, which reached out over fifty miles. When an island appears on the horizon in those vast distances of the sea, it is truly a cause to stop and consider the history and geography of a unique entity. I will confess as a ship captain deviating a bit from a planned track simply to sail by one of these islands to break the relentless monotony of a deployment, and to point out to the crew the small spot of civilization in our path, reminding them that there is land after all, in the midst of the "water world" we were encompassing.

The list of islands in the book is organized by world ocean, so it begins appropriately at the top of the world with the islands of the Arctic Ocean, of which there are only three. Then, in order, the Atlantic (with nine islands), Indian (seven islands), and Pacific Oceans. The latter supplies us with over half of the islands in the collection (twenty-seven), which makes perfect sense given its vast size. A way to think about the size of the Pacific Ocean is that you could take all the land on earth and drop it comfortably into the Pacific Ocean with space left over. Finally, the Antarctic Ocean appears with the remaining four islands in the collection. Each of them has a vibrant story that is naturally tied almost entirely to the sea and the mariners that discovered, colonized, and fought over these unique entities.

Everyone, experienced mariner and landsman alike, will be particularly struck by one or two islands as you dip in and out of this small, handy volume. For me, three of note would be Pitcairn and Easter Islands in the Pacific and Tristan da Cunha in the south Atlantic. Many will recognize the name Pitcairn Island as the destination of the mutineers in the often-retold story of the mutiny on HMS *Bounty*. After leaving the ship, nine mutineers and their Tahitian captives made their way to this tiny island in 1790. It remains a British territory today, with a population of around fifty descendants.

Easter Island is likewise located in what some have called "the desert of the Pacific" and is owned by Chile. The famous large stone statues, nearly a thousand in number, dot the coastline. The archeological mystery surrounding the population and the meaning of the statues remain. While better known than most of these islands, its origins remain shrouded in the mystery of the sea. And, finally, in the far south of the Atlantic is Tristan da Cunha, a British possession that was a utopian colony in the early 1800s run by an eccentric Scotsman, William Glass. Today it has about 250 inhabitants and no airstrip—it is a six-day sail to the island from "nearby" South Africa. To Navy sailors, two additional well-known islands are Diego Garcia (an atoll that is a military base in the Indian Ocean) and Iwo Jima (sight of a massive, famous battle in World War II). And even modestly well-informed historians will know Saint Helena in the deep Atlantic as the final exile of Napoleon and his death place.

But the real treasures of this book are the islands virtually no one has even heard of—islands named Semisopochnoi, Takuu, Banaba, Rapa Iti, Atlasov, Antpodes, Possession, Pagan, Laurie, South Keeling, Tromelin, and on and on. What links them together, of course, is the sea. And these strange, small places broke the horizon for sailors over centuries. Reading the *Atlas of Remote Islands* is a voyage to nowhere in some ways, but in others, a story of man's determination to sail to the furthest corners of the world.

Bonus: *Early Sea Charts* by Robert Putnam is an oversized, full-color, absolutely gorgeous atlas of seventy-six of the most beautiful of early sea charts and maps.[3] Ranging from the earliest hand-produced and painted examples from the 1300s to the early 1700s, the volume focuses on the "golden age of exploration" in the 1500s and 1600s. On these charts appear for the first time in history some of the fifty islands in Judith Schalansky's work, and having the two books side by side is like returning to that distant time of discovery.

CHAPTER THREE

COD
A Biography of the Fish that Changed the World

by Mark Kurlansky

The codfish lays a thousand eggs,
The homely hen lays one.
The codfish never cackles
To tell you what she's done.
And so we scorn the codfish
While the humble hen we prize
Which only goes to show you
That it pays to advertise.

—Anonymous American rhyme[1]

In another life I would have been a cook. Not a "chef," mind you, but some-one who could run the line at a small bistro. I grew up around cooks and hearty cooking, learned the skills early, and continue to make all manner of Mediterranean dishes nightly—risotto, paella, tagine, cassoulet, pasta sauces, and of course any kind of Greek dish. My grandfather emigrated to the United States and opened a small diner here, like many Greek Americans. His was called the Downtown Diner and was about the size of the small restaurant immortalized in the film *My Big Fat Greek Wedding*. They did a lot of roast chicken, cheeseburgers, lasagna, spaghetti, stews, and soups. Not fancy, but filling. I'm told one of the most popular dishes was the fish chowder, which featured fresh cod. You could stand a spoon up in the chowder, it was so thick and rich not only with the fish but potatoes, onions, and bacon and garnished with parsley.

Taking that cod fixation forward, when I was teaching *Moby-Dick* at Tufts University in the mid-1980s as part of a class on literature of the sea, I would make a couple of different kinds of chowder for my classes each semester—typically a pot of clam chowder, but the real star of those evenings was the cod chowder. As wonderful and utilitarian as it is, cod chowder is only one of a seemingly infinite number of ways to prepare this wonderful, meaty fish. Mark Kurlansky's neat little book *Cod: The Biography of the Fish that Changed the World* is full of anecdotes, history, war, geopolitics, and—yes, indeed—recipes. In fact the final part of the book is "six centuries of cod recipes." The hunger that mankind feels for the cod is reflected in the variety of the recipes: English fish and chips, New England cod chowder, Basque bacalao a la Vizcaina, Portuguese fish stew, French bouillabaisse, and on and on.

As we learn in *Cod*, all that demand has a cost, and a significant one. In a word, the cost is overfishing. This is a fish that numbered in the millions and millions as recently as mid-twentieth century in the Greenland–Iceland–United Kingdom "gap," where the nuclear submarines of the Cold War once sailed. Cod can be a big fish, and a thriving one—but today it is virtually extinct in many parts of traditional fishing grounds. Its demise is the end of what Kurlansky calls, "a 1,000-year fishing spree," going back to the Vikings who chased the fish all the way to North America in their day.[2] Of note, the Vikings discovered how to dry the fish out by hanging it in the fresh, dry winter air, then use it as preserved rations on their long voyages. They also began to trade it south to European markets, triggering the demand that has led to the current challenges.

The Basques learned the art of salt curing the fish, and many recipes revolve around taking the salted fish, bacalao, and rehydrating it while removing the incipient salt. By the middle of the 1500s, over half of the fish eaten in Europe was cod, pulled from the Atlantic by coastal fishermen from England and the Nordic countries south through France and Spain. The first of the "cod wars"— and there have been many, lingering on to the present day—was fought in the 1530s between England and the Hanseatic League of the Baltic seacoast. We also learn the history of the "codpiece" much used by medieval men to cosmetically exaggerate the size of the genital areas.

The cod is a hearty fish, swimming mouth-wide-open and hoovering up pretty much anything that will fit down its gullet. But it began to dwindle in the twentieth century because of efficiencies that emerged in the fishing industry—freezing fish, stronger nets, powered-lines to pull the brimming nets, sonar to find the big groups swimming together. The cod never had a chance.

The book is Mark Kurlansky's third, and he's gone on to write other fascinating books, including one that is the world history of salt. He's the kind of distinctive writer who can make anything interesting, much like John McPhee's *Looking for a Ship*, about the life of merchant seamen. Kurlansky is a journalist who has written convincingly (and entertainingly) about not only cod and salt; his books also highlight the story of milk, salmon, and paper. He follows the tale of cod more or less chronologically and along the way provides insight into the "followers of the cod" and their life and times. We meet the Vikings, Basque, English, Spanish, French, and many others who are all pursuing the fish. In chapter 6, "A Cod War Heard Round the World," Kurlansky lays out the role of fishing competition between the United States and Britain, both at the time of the American Revolution and later in the War of 1812. He drills in on the "Cod Wars," which mainly occurred from 1958 to 1972 between Iceland and the United Kingdom but continue to this day (fortunately no serious shots have been fired between the two NATO allies). Chapter 9 focuses on the Icelanders, perhaps the hardiest of the fishing nations, and their conflict with northern European nations. Indeed, the two themes of the book are the at-one-time-robust seagoing life of the cod posited against all the abuse man can pile against it.

These controversies have hardly lessened in the more than two decades since Kurlansky published *Cod*. As I write this amid the COVID-19 pandemic of mid-2020, the story in Europe is when and how the British will finally achieve the Brexit they voted for three years ago. And alongside the ongoing arguments about the Irish border and the integration (or not) of Northern Ireland with both

Great Britain and the European Union, the other remaining stumbling point is—you guessed it—fishing rights for EU nations and Britain. The concerns that Kurlansky raises about cod and the north Atlantic have become part of the larger conversation about the rising temperatures of the oceans and illegal fishing all around the world ocean. This is a highly readable book, way ahead of its time, and its clever portrait of the cod—both in geopolitics and in the dinner pot— deserves a spot on *The Sailor's Bookshelf.*

Bonus: *The Cod's Tale,* also by Mark Kurlansky, is a children's book published in 2001. It is a clever and beautifully illustrated tale, replete with lovely maps. It fits nicely alongside *Cod.*

CHAPTER FOUR

DEEP

Freediving, Renegade Science, and What the Ocean Tells Us about Ourselves

by James Nestor

The sea remains the final unseen, untouched,
and undiscovered wilderness, the planet's last
great frontier. All the stress, noise and distractions
of life are left at the surface. The ocean is the
last truly quiet place on Earth.[1]

I am but an indifferent swimmer, capable enough of getting from one end of the pool to the other and staying afloat in the deep end with a young grandchild clinging to my neck. But when I venture into the ocean, somehow the whole idea of merging into the sea starts to take over. The natural buoyancy of salt water is part of that, of course, but so in the primeval bond between humans and the ocean. Can it be only a coincidence that the percentage of water in our bodies—about 70 percent—is roughly the same as the percentage of seawater covering the earth? Or that around 70 percent of the oxygen that we breathe comes from photosynthesis in the ocean? With all due respect to former vice president and global environmentalist Al Gore, it is not the Amazon that is the "lungs of the earth," as important as it is—it is the oceans. They call to us.

As James Nestor points out in this fascinating book, "We are born of the oceans. Each of us begins life floating in amniotic fluid that has almost the same makeup as ocean water. Our earliest characteristics are fishlike. The month-old embryo grows fins first, not feet; it is one misfiring gene away from developing fins instead of hands. At the fifth week of a fetus's development, its heart has two chambers, a characteristic shared by fish."[2] Kevin Costner, in the strange but oddly compelling film *Waterworld*, has a big physical reveal early in the story: he possesses gills. Infants can instinctively breaststroke underwater (don't test that theory at home, please) and know how to hold their breath underwater. There are deep bonds, pun intended, between humans and the sea.[3] Nestor, who had never seen the international sport known as "freediving" before covering a competition one summer in Greece, sets out to show the reader this bond, and he succeeds brilliantly. As you read *Deep*, you yearn to get to a beach and into the ocean.

Freediving is probably the cheapest and simplest sport imaginable. It requires the diver to hold his or her breath while achieving the deepest level possible in the ocean. At the most basic level, freediving is descending (a whale would say "sounding") as deeply as you can without any form of scuba gear. Take a deep breath and start swimming straight down in the ocean and you are freediving. Since most adults can hold their breath comfortably for only around a minute or so (I just tested myself and was gasping by ninety seconds), it is quite remarkable to learn that exceptional freedivers can stay down for more than ten minutes. It is a matter of training, experience, and basic physiology (some people simply have larger lung capacity, or their muscles operate without oxygen more efficiently).

Naturally, it is not simply the lack of oxygen that is challenging when freediving deeply—it is also the pressure and temperature. As a freediver goes deeper into the sea, gliding downward beyond thirty feet, pressure begins to act on the human body in profound ways. Often, freedivers can experience blackouts, nosebleeds, damage to their lungs, and decompression sickness (commonly called "the bends") as they come back up. The pressure on the body, particularly on the lungs, is profound, squeezing them down to something the size of a couple of baseballs at great depths. Nestor spends time with extreme athletes and the slightly "renegade" scientists who are deeply embedded in the sport. Along the way, he also discovers the sonic communications of whales, the manner in which sharks navigate (often below two thousand feet, in the blackest and coldest waters), the way swimming without any gear changes interactions with marine life, and above all the effects on the human body the deeper it goes. He is an engaging writer, and reading the book is indeed like diving into the sea.

In addition to the international competitive freediving activities, there are underwater versions of football, spearfishing contests, rugby, hockey, target shooting, and snorkeling. The beauty of synchronized swimming depends to some degree on what is essentially freediving and breath-holding. And freediving is not merely recreational sport; it is a regulated circuit of high-end competition. For competitive freediving, there are a couple of world associations monitoring what is at heart a very dangerous sport. Even Nestor's book has a disclaimer at the beginning, saying the volume is not meant to "teach" freediving and should not be used to learn the sport, an attempt to absolve the author of any liability. As with most sports, what began as very simple competition—just dive down and see how far you can go—has become complicated and broken into individual disciplines. There are world records in simple breath-holding while floating (over eleven minutes); diving with and without either dual fins or monofins; distance swum in a pool without breathing; freediving with and without weights, and so on. The deepest dive I could find was nine hundred feet, which is pretty deep even for a military submarine.

Many cultures have participated in some form of freediving for centuries, going back to ancient Greek sponge divers and Japanese "ama" divers, collecting pearls from the ocean floor. Nestor takes the reader neatly and swiftly through all of this as well as the basics of the sport, its history, and the contemporary culture. The heart of the book is twofold: Nestor's experiences learning to freedive at a competent level, and the endless pull of the ocean on each of us. Should you take up the sport? I'd say be careful. Nestor talks about a 2013 fatality of a diver who was less experienced and pushed himself too hard. Dive only with a "dive buddy," practice breath control on land first, build gradually to permit your muscles to work with less or no oxygen. This is not an activity for the faint of heart, quite literally. But as Nestor continually points out, it is an activity that taps into the deepest impulses of human psyche and touches some elements of our physiology and psychology in profound ways. *Deep* is the wettest book on *The Sailor's Bookshelf* and offers a truly unique connection to the sea.

Bonus: *Waterworld*, the visually stunning and highly creative film with Kevin Costner as "the mariner," is an unexpected delight. Set in the year 2500 after the polar ice has all melted, it is a glimpse of what life could look like with the entire planet covered by water. As much as I love the sea, that is not the world I want, but as an environmental cautionary tale and pretty good entertainment, it is worth a watch as you read *Deep.*

CHAPTER FIVE

LONGITUDE
The True Story of a Lone Genius Who Solved the Greatest Scientific Problem of His Time

by Dava Sobel

A boat ride down the Thames from Westminster to Greenwich is a tour through time.

—Neil Armstrong[1]

From 2009 to 2013, I was the first admiral to serve as the Supreme Allied Commander of NATO, following a long line of generals stretching back to the first commander, Dwight Eisenhower. There were many wonderful parts of the job, but one thing I particularly enjoyed was the opportunity to visit the many nations of NATO and our partner countries. And because I was the first mariner in the job, people would often show me aspects of their nation's seafaring history. One of the most memorable of all my visits was to the National Maritime Museum at Greenwich, England, where I was able to see everything from a uniform worn by Vice Adm. Lord Nelson before his death at the epic battle of Trafalgar, to the charts actually handled by Capt. James Cook, perhaps the greatest of ocean explorers.

But the highlight of the visit was actually seeing something that sounds prosaic—a collection of clocks from the eighteenth century. They were clustered together in Flamsteed House, an observatory built in the late 1600s during the reign of King Charles II. This was not just any bunch of old clocks, of course, but rather the first truly accurate set of marine chronometers. They were built by a former carpenter named John Harrison and consisted of increasingly smaller clocks, descending in dimensions from over two feet per side for the first clock down to the fourth version, which looked a bit like a pocket watch and was about six inches in diameter. When you look at those chronometers, you are truly looking at the keys to the age of exploration—essential to the ability to accurately find yourself on the earth's surface. How these devices came to exist and the changes they rendered in the long story of mankind's voyage on the oceans is the story that Dava Sobel unwinds brilliantly in Longitude.

For many centuries, navigators were able to determine how far north and south they were on the globe—that is, the latitude—with reasonable accuracy. The problem was knowing how far east or west a ship was from a known location, or the longitude. Latitude is far easier to determine because you can fix your position by shooting the sun during the day and the moon and planets at night with a simple sextant. This allows you to easily "measure" where you are on the face of planet Earth north or south of the equator. With longitude, because of the earth's rapid rotation on its essentially vertical axis, no such easy reference points exist.

As a result, navigators could not sail with a great deal of accuracy, resulting over the centuries in many terrible and unnecessary shipwrecks or prolonged voyages after "missing a turn" so to speak. This became extremely vexing as the European powers continued to sail globally, and especially so as the desire to trade across the oceans and control distant colonies became drivers of global geopolitics in the 1600s.

As a result, the British Parliament offered a financial reward of 20,000 pounds (the equivalent of $5 million in 2020 U.S. dollars) to anyone who could solve the "longitude problem." John Harrison, a gifted craftsman, accepted the challenge believing that the best solution (as opposed to using some form of astral navigation) was to build a highly accurate chronometer (the term for a maritime clock) that could withstand the rigors of a shipboard environment. He did exactly that over decades in the mid-1700s, creating first large sea clocks (known as H-1, H-2, and H-3) and finally his masterpiece, the so-called sea watch, or H-4. The latter chronometer was really a watch, not much bigger than a large pocket watch. He worked assiduously with the Board of Longitude, some members of which were skeptical of his work, notably the Reverend Nevil Maskelyne, who was a devout believer in a celestial observation solution.

A prolonged series of trials were arranged for the "sea watch," and—unfortunately for Harrison—Maskelyne was able to exert a great deal of negative influence over the results of the watch trials. By 1765 the "sea watch" had gained enough of a following, however, to win an offer from Parliament for a 10,000-pound award. But Harrison's nemesis, Maskelyne, had become the Astronomer Royal and remained at least partially in the driver's seat as a member of the Board of Longitude. The antipathy between the two men was intense. Eventually Harrison was able to obtain an audience with King George III and won him over through a trial in the palace of his latest "sea watch," the H-5. With support from the crown and yet another petition to Parliament, Harrison was finally able to receive nearly 9,000 pounds of the remaining prize money, although he was formerly denied the title of prizewinner. By this time he was over eighty years old and only lived a few more years.

As a young midshipman at Annapolis, I first learned to use a sextant and worked through the rudiments of navigation. To do so, I used the *Nautical Almanac*, essentially a compilation of celestial data compiled by the U.S. and British navies, which had been originated and championed by Maskelyne, ironically. I have "shot" the sun and the stars many, many times, but the advent first of electronic aids to navigation and then, of course, of today's Global Positioning Systems (GPS) has rendered locating your position on the earth a trivial exercise. Anyone can pick up a smart phone and know within a few feet where on earth they stand. Ah, but those beautiful chronometers tick on in Greenwich, a distant echo of John Harrison's brilliance and craftsmanship. In *Longitude*, Dava Sobel has given us a short but detailed story of solving one of the great technical challenges that sailors faced nearly three hundred years ago. And if those GPS satellites are ever hacked, let's hope sailors can still find both their latitude *and* longitude.

CHAPTER SIX

DUTTON'S NAUTICAL NAVIGATION, 15TH EDITION

by Thomas J. Cutler

From its earliest days, navigation has
been both an art and a science.[1]

W hen I arrived at Annapolis to join the U.S. Naval Academy's class of 1976 in the hot and humid summer of 1972, I had zero knowledge of navigation. While I had been at sea few times as a child either on the way to Greece or sailing the Aegean on tourist boats, I had certainly never set foot on the bridge of a ship of any kind, or been in a sailing craft. And frankly, I wasn't overly interested in learning to navigate or sail because I had set out to the Naval Academy to become a U.S. Marine infantry officer like my father. So I looked at learning both to sail and to navigate as necessary and annoying aspects of getting through the four years of the Academy before heading to the Marines. As anyone who has glanced at my biography knows, that is not how things turned out.

As I've described elsewhere, that idea of being a ground-pounding Marine began to change in the summer of 1973 when I stepped on the bridge of a warship for the first time aboard USS *Jouett*, sailing out of San Diego bound for Hawaii on a summer "midshipman's cruise." As I stood the basic watches of a midshipman, third class, I learned to steer the ship using the helm on the bridge; to manipulate the engines down below using the engine order telegraph, also on the bridge; to rig signal flags while standing watch "up in the wind" with the signalmen; and to understand some very basic navigational skills, really just the use of a pelorus (a device used to take bearings) and a bit of chart-pricking with dividers to calculate a distance on a track. When my classmates and I came back from our summer cruises, one of the classes we took that fall, unlike pretty much any other college sophomore in America, was navigation.

I was lucky that my instructor of that first semester of navigation was among the very best at the Academy in the mid-1970s: a Royal Navy officer named Richard A. Smith. He eventually became president of the International Association of Institutes of Navigation and served thirty-five years in the British navy. Rising up from an ordinary seaman to become a captain, he headed the department of navigation at Annapolis and held the navigation desk at the U.K. Ministry of Defense. It was great fortune to be in the section he taught, and he literally made navigation, in all its complexity and scientific basis and richness, come alive. He was also an internationally recognized expert on the rules of the nautical road and edited several books on that highly nuanced and legalistic subject. One of the books he championed in the teaching of the course was a later edition of Benjamin Dutton's classic 1926 book, *Navigation and Piloting*. Captain Smith was also well acquainted with an even earlier corresponding classic, Nathaniel Bowditch's *The American Practical Navigator*, first published in 1802. Of the two, I've chosen Dutton's as more approachable for those not as fully engaged with the sea. Dutton's was certainly the text I turned to again and again over long years at sea.

The new edition is beautifully edited by retired Navy lieutenant commander Tom Cutler, the author or editor of many fine books maritime affairs. He brings more than forty years of experience in virtually every aspect of marine operations to bear, reflecting his service in every size of Navy warship, from patrol boats to aircraft carriers. Among his many other books are *Brown Water, Black Berets: Coastal and Riverine Warfare in Vietnam* (2000) and *The Battle of Leyte Gulf: 23–26 October 1944* (1994). He was the executive assistant to the chair of the navigation and seamanship department at Annapolis and "teacher of the year" there in 1988–89. He is also a friend and shipmate of mine for over thirty years, and there is no one whose nautical judgment and thorough seamanship I respect more.

In Tom's capable hands, this fifteenth edition of *Dutton's Nautical Navigation* begins simply with understanding the problems in finding position on a sphere like the earth. Anyone can follow his clear descriptions of latitude (the lines that go sideways) and longitude (the ones that go up and down). How the equator and poles fit into the challenge of positioning and the difference between a great circle or a rhumb line course on a chart become clear. After establishing a baseline of knowledge, he begins with the simplest instrument in navigation—a piece of paper, also known as a "chart." (Maps are of land areas, charts are depictions of the sea and coastal areas.) Very quickly the reader gains an understanding of the differences in charts, how to find and purchase them, what all of the small images on them mean (e.g., a compass rose, symbols for buoys and lights). From there it is a quick leap to the use of electronic media, notably electronic charts. The Navy recently reverted to using both electronic and paper charts, a wise decision given the ability of opponents to attack the ubiquitous but highly vulnerable Global Positioning System through satellite or cyberattacks.

Chapters continue with descriptions of nautical publications (tidal charts, for example); aids to navigation such as lights and buoys and how to use them in finding position; and the mysteries of the nautical compass. A chapter on navigational equipment follows, to include use of an azimuth circle, a pelorus, dividers to measure distance on a chart, a stadimeter to discern distance over the sea, parallel rulers, and of course a sextant. Only now, after inculcating the basics, does the reader begin to read about actual techniques of navigation itself, starting with dead reckoning—simply tracking the ship along a course plotted on the chart.

Understanding tides and their effect on navigation follows, as does their close cousin, currents. Piloting, radar navigation, use of GPS, and finally navigational astronomy emerge. To perform the latter, of course, it is necessary to know the constellations of stars in the sky—all of that far easier today with simple and free aps that provide the info, but Dutton's lays out how it all works.

Chapter 22, "The Sextant," is superb and lays out in simple detail but professional depth the way to use that most primal of all navigational tools. The final third of the book is largely a crisp and clear discussion of how to use celestial navigation. The volume concludes with some specialized aspects of navigation, including both polar and lifeboat navigational challenges. I recently reread the chapter on lifeboat navigation in preparation for reviewing both *Men against the Sea* from the "Bounty Trilogy" and *In the Heart of the Sea* for *The Sailor's Bookshelf*, as both are stories of epic navigational challenges for survivors from nineteenth-century catastrophes at sea (the former the mutiny on the *Bounty* and the latter the destruction of the whaleship *Essex*).

There is a plethora of books on the market about how to navigate at sea, but Dutton's is the gold standard. Whether the reader is an experienced mariner refreshing herself for an offshore sailing voyage down the east coast of the United States or someone seeking to simply understand the "art and science" of navigation, Dutton's can make all of mankind's long quest to know where they are on the trackless ocean make sense.

Bonus: As mentioned above, the competing volume—more dense, older, somehow more traditional—is Bowditch's 1802 *American Practical Navigator*, which is worth skimming, if only to see the evolution of the work (and of navigation) after two centuries. Also relevant and from *The Sailor's Bookshelf* is Dava Sobel's brief but highly readable *Longitude*, on how sailors finally solved the longitude problem after centuries of efforts.

CHAPTER SEVEN

NAVAL SHIPHANDLER'S GUIDE

by Capt. James A. Barber Jr., USN (Ret.)

Shiphandling is both a science and an art.[1]

There is nothing more fundamental to humankind's relationship with the seas than the ability to safely and smartly handle a ship. The term itself is instructive: we don't *drive* a ship. We *handle* the ship, implying a certain tenderness, a need to be careful with its delicate and thin skin, so easily bruised and torn by offending bulkheads, icebergs, ramming implements from other warships, and the thousand other dangers that threaten a hull. It is a measure by which the skill and professionalism of any mariner are assessed, whether she is teenager steering a small sailing dingy out of a slip on a calm summer's day or he is a grizzled civilian master guiding his massive cargo carrier through the tight confines of the Panama Canal. For naval officers in the surface line in particular, it is a fundamental professional skill that requires deep attention, study, review, and practice to master.

I was lucky as a junior officer to serve in a new type of destroyer, the *Spruance* class, named after the acclaimed World War II admiral Raymond Spruance. The ships were fitted out with four gas turbine engines and twin rudders and screws and were highly responsive to the commands of the shiphandler on the bridge, which were smoothly transmitted to the engineering spaces. My first captain was a very experienced shiphandler himself, somewhat volatile in his teaching methods, but over the course of several years I improved to the point that I was eventually nominated for the Pacific Fleet "shiphandler of the year" award (which I did not win, sadly). At the end of that tour, I also wrote the first of a series of articles I would pen for the U.S. Naval Institute *Proceedings* magazine on how to handle a *Spruance*-class destroyer. Subsequently I would write about handling a *Ticonderoga*-class cruiser (a bigger, more complex platform), then finally an *Arleigh Burke*–class destroyer, the most numerous class of ship in the U.S. Navy today.[2]

Indeed, I have always loved the feeling of giving a rudder command in the open ocean to a big, fast-responding warship and, as the vessel heels in response to the rudder and engines, you can look out of the bridge wing windows and feel as though it is not just the ship that is moving but the entire vast horizon of the oceans. For anyone with their hand on the tiller of even a tiny sailboat or the wheel and throttle of a high-powered speedboat, the feelings are the same. When you handle a ship, and do it well, you are part of a long line of mariners that stretches back to the very beginnings of man's voyage on the sea. To know the sea means to understand the power and glory of steering a vessel.

Capt. Jim Barber, the author of this volume, was a beautiful shiphandler himself. I met him in the late 1970s when he was a senior captain in command of the cruiser *Horne*, deploying in the same Carrier Battle Group in which I was serving in my *Spruance*. His ship was noted for the professional, smooth way in which he handled her, and in barroom conversations with the junior officers in his ship from Hong Kong to Subic Bay, I heard again and again that he was a careful, thoughtful, and natural teacher to the younger officers under his command. That's the kind of captain to have, and when I got to know Captain Barber later in my career (we served together on the board of the U.S. Naval Institute, where he was for years the chief executive officer), I always found him to be a kind, empathetic, and balanced leader. He personified the view that the way in which a mariner handles a ship speaks volumes about their personality and leadership skills.

This book is a follow-on to a couple of earlier classics, although it supersedes both in laying out the skills of shiphandling. Both Knight's *Modern Seamanship*, most recently revised by Capt. John V. Noel Jr., and *Naval Shiphandling* by Capt. R. S. Crenshaw are worthy books, and I cut my teeth on them as an ensign. But Jim Barber has vastly deepened and improved both, offering fundamental lessons in practical shiphandling for naval officers while simultaneously laying out for landsmen what this "art and science" is really about.

The book is organized in roughly the order of events that a mariner will encounter in handling a ship. He begins with how to learn shiphandling ashore in a high-tech, modern simulator. These, by the way, are *very* realistic. While in refresher training to be a destroyer captain for the first time, I nearly forgot that my simulated ship was merely a projection on the wall when I approached a pier too swiftly. Barber then talks about the physics of shiphandling, laying out the various forces—wind, current, the Bernoulli principle and Venturi effect, engines, rudders, lines to the pier—that can impact how the ship actually moves through the water. In this introductory section, he closes with the "standard commands" that shiphandlers use when directing the rudder and engines of the ship, for example, "full speed ahead," "right standard rudder," "all back full," and so on.

The heart of this book is a series of chapters that provide a shiphandler—whether a brand-new mariner or a very experienced ship captain in need of a review—concise, meaningful directions in maneuvering the ship through its various paces. Barber begins, logically, with getting under way—perhaps the easiest of shiphandling maneuvers where you have a maximum degree of control. Then come chapters on how to make a safe landing (I've had my share of botched ones, believe me); using the anchors and other ground tackle (mooring devices); transiting a channel; and underway replenishment (pulling up alongside another naval vessel at sea to transfer stores, ammunition, or personnel—a somewhat dangerous operation). As you read the book, you really feel you are gradually getting under way and heading out to sea.

One of the best chapters discusses the role of tugs and a pilot. The degree to which a mariner uses such aides varies greatly by class of ship, procedures of the governing organization, and the personality of the captain. In my case, I always took full advantage, requesting two tugs (one fore and another aft) and an experienced pilot to advise me. None of that would ever absolve a captain of his or her responsibility for handling the ship, or for any damage or mistake that occurred. But it seemed to me foolish not to take advantage of all the assistance available.

Never put your ego ahead of your ship's safety, is my view. Yet I've known other captains, often very good ones, who chose to eschew the use of tugs or even the advice of a pilot. Their reasoning seemed to be that no one knew their ship better than they did, from the responsiveness of the engines to the skill of the deck force in getting lines over, and thus *they* would be the best judge of how to best bring the ship into port and alongside. Perhaps. But I will take that offered edge, keep it in my back pocket, bring my own skill to the table, but be unafraid to ask for a helpful nudge from a tug or a word of advice from an old pilot—who probably makes more landings in a year than I did in my entire career.

This marvelous book concludes with some "special advice" tied to the characteristics of all of the major classes of ships in the fleet today. While this is a bit specific for U.S. naval officers, the broad advice that shines through is valuable to anyone seeking an understanding of the skill of handling a ship, especially in high-pressure situations. Of note, each of the chapters in the book begins with a short "sea story" that illuminates some particularly trenchant point. Those alone are worth the price of admission as they reflect the skill and heart of a fine sea captain, Jim Barber. His gift for teaching—honed during his three warship commands, his attainment of a prestigious PhD ashore, and his fifteen-year leadership of the U.S. Naval Institute—is here on full and valuable display.

CHAPTER EIGHT

SEA POWER
A Naval History

edited by E. B. Potter and Chester W. Nimitz

As Britain for centuries stood off Western Europe, and maintained the balance of power therein, largely by means of her Royal Navy, so the United States now stands at the very center of the world's sea power complex, maintaining the balance of power in the rest of the world.

—Fleet Adm. Chester Nimitz[1]

When I was a first-year student at the U.S. Naval Academy in 1972, every "plebe," as we were called, was required to take a full-year course called simply "Sea Power." This fundamental building block of a naval officer's education was taught to all 1,200 in my incoming class (just under 900 would eventually graduate four years later, by the way). In order to run so many individual sections of about 25 midshipmen, of course, there needed to be a bevy of teachers. Most were junior officers in the Navy or Marine Corps, often on their first shore assignment after three or four years of sea duty following their own commissioning. Many were themselves recent Annapolis grads, and most were self-taught as historians but managed to do a reasonable job of slogging through the material of the course. But I was lucky—my small section that first semester was taught by the professor who had literally "written the book" on sea power: E. B. "Ned" Potter.

Professor Potter was the leading teacher of naval history at Annapolis, starting from the late 1940s. He arrived at the Academy following three years of sea duty with the U.S. Pacific Fleet from 1943 to the end of the war in 1945. After demobilizing, he returned to the Academy as a civilian and stayed there teaching for the rest of a long and productive career. In addition to editing both the first and second editions of *Sea Power*, the first in conjunction with legendary Fleet Adm. Chester Nimitz, he also wrote well-received biographies of a group of World War II Navy leaders: Fleet Admiral Nimitz (1976); Fleet Adm. William "Bull" Halsey (1985); and Adm. Arleigh Burke (1990). But the greatest and most enduring of his works was *Sea Power*.

In the forward to the first edition, published in 1960, Potter wrote, "'Sea Power' is in a sense four books in one: a history of the United States Navy and of American naval power; a history of the world's navies; a study of the evolution of naval warfare; and a study of the part that sea power has played in the exercise of national power." That first edition is hard to find, but if you obtain one, hold on to it, for it is truly a classic. At 932 pages, the book is hardly a one-night read, but it can be enjoyably consumed over time. It is also not written from a single pen but rather is a collective effort organized by Potter and encouraged by Nimitz, that ultimately included dozens of writers of varying backgrounds and experiences. Yet the genius of Potter as the overarching editor, backed by the steady engagement of the iconic Fleet Admiral, has produced a volume that in fact reads very much in a single, smooth tone. It also benefits from the extraordinary access Nimitz enjoyed to every senior naval commander in World War II, and the portion of the book devoted to that conflict is the equal of any book written on the sweeping naval engagements of that time. It is also full of dozens of maps, charts, and, above all, detailed tactical depictions of individual battles, the latter ranging from the Bay of Salamis, where the Greeks and Persians fought 2,500 years ago, through Trafalgar at the height of the Napoleonic Wars, to the pivotal battles of Midway and Leyte Gulf in World War II.

Some of my Annapolis classmates may have called the course "Z-Power," as in "zzz" for falling asleep, but I loved it and was inspired by it, especially that first semester with Professor Potter himself. He balanced lecture with discussion, and over the course of the semester (and ultimately the second semester as well), the key themes of the course emerged: (1) the influence of sea power upon history (echoing the key ideas of Alfred Thayer Mahan); (2) the reasoning behind strategic decisions at sea; (3) the characteristics of successful leadership (with many anecdotes about Navy admirals); (4) the evolution of naval weapons (in many places quite technical, from sail to steam to torpedoes to radar and sonar); (5) the evolution of naval tactics; and (6) the evolution of amphibious doctrine (and the key partnership of the Navy and Marine Corps).[2]

What is also evident in this fine book is a sense of the vital strategic importance of the oceans. Again and again, while unpacking the key naval battles of history—Salamis, Lepanto, Yorktown, Trafalgar, Jutland, Midway, the Battle of the Atlantic, and Leyte Gulf, among many others—we see how the sea has shaped the really big outcomes in human history. After Fleet Admiral Nimitz died, Professor Potter did a second edition, which remains in print today, and can easily be obtained from the U.S. Naval Institute, which took over the project. Like the first edition, the second is a group project, and it was that second, much shorter edition that I studied at Annapolis. My battered copy is signed by Professor Potter, and I treasure it. But that first edition, at nearly twice the length, is the better bargain. When I set out to write my own book about the oceans, *Sea Power: The History and Geopolitics of the World's Oceans*, I gladly dipped into both editions of *Sea Power*. My own book takes a different tack and looks at the seas on an ocean-by-ocean basis. Immodestly, perhaps, I believe it is a good book but different in tone and style than the classic by Potter and Nimitz. I am lucky to have been a student of E. B. Potter; following his death in 1997, I took down the signed second edition and read it all through again. It is a fine way to sail through the seas of history.

Bonus: For a complementary take on sea power, may I have the audacity to recommend my own aforementioned book? It was published by Penguin Press / Random House in 2017. I think my old professor would be proud that I picked the name I did, an homage to all he taught me and generations of naval officers.

CHAPTER NINE

THE HUNGRY OCEAN
A Swordboat Captain's Journey

by Linda Greenlaw

This is the first symptom of sea fever: a passion for
bluer waters and bigger fish.[1]

First and foremost, this is a compelling, well-written, occasionally funny, and at times very moving book—it just happens to be about fishing, but it is the humanity and leadership skills of Linda Greenlaw that carry the book. She became semifamous (at least in the maritime world) when she had an important cameo role in Sebastian Junger's superb and gritty book *The Perfect Storm*. In the movie adaptation of the book, her role is played by Mary Elizabeth Mastrantonio. Greenlaw was the only woman swordboat captain on the East Coast and, according to some, among the very top captains in the fishing fleet. She freely admits, by the way, that during the storm depicted in *The Perfect Storm*, she was actually six hundred nautical miles to the west of the boat that sank, *Andrea Gail*. She and the skipper of *Andrea Gail* were friendly rivals, and Greenlaw was the last to speak to the doomed boat on the radio.

Greenlaw is easy to like. Born and raised in New England, she was always deeply attracted to the sea and spent long summers boating in every conceivable kind of small craft out of Isle au Haut, a small village on an island off the Maine coast. After attending Colby College in Maine, she began serious fishing, first as a deckhand (and often the cook, a vital role on any small fishing boat). Eventually, she worked her way up to swordboat captain in 1986. After her small costar-turn in *The Perfect Storm*, she decided to undertake her other passion—writing. She has now published three books about being a fishing boat captain (both swordfish and lobster). Additionally, she has published a couple of cookbooks and a moving memoir about adopting a daughter late in life. Of late, she has created a fictional character who is a kind of marine investigator-detective, Jane Bunker. Her books are all readable, but the crown jewel is the first, *The Hungry Ocean*, which—improbably enough, given its esoteric subject matter—made it near the top of the *New York Times* bestseller lists.

In the *The Hungry Ocean*, the tragedy of *Andrea Gail* is years in the past, although never far from Greenlaw's mind. But this is entirely the story of a sister ship, *Hannah Boden*, following a single swordfish fishing trip from start to finish—with a few vignettes from earlier in her life (called "Mug Ups," after a fisherman's term for a coffee break). The first thing that shines through is simple: her love of fishing and the deep ocean. As she says, "The next morning, big, white, cumulus clouds drifted eastward, selfishly interrupting the sun's light, which had traveled so far to warm the decks of the [ship]. But the sun was persistent and broke through holes in the clouds resulting in vertical columns of multi-colored light that landed in bright yellow splotches in the sea around us."[2]

Alongside an appreciation of the beauty of her world, she also masterfully illuminates how *hard* the task of fishing is for the crew of her ship. It is a rough, demanding, and harsh life at sea, especially in these small boats. One chapter begins: "Three crew members and I watched with interest as a fourth man extracted his own tooth with a needle nosed pliers."[3] She also deals with racism, exhaustion, significant illness, and a couple of deaths by the end of the book. Despite being the only woman skipper in the fleet, she quickly and convincingly dismisses gender challenges: "Being a woman hasn't been a big deal. I never anticipated problems stemming from being female, and never encountered any." Her explanation: "I might be thick-skinned—or just too damn busy working to worry about what others might think of me."[4]

As the captain, she has the same sense of loneliness that any sea captain faces, from a Joseph Conrad "secret sharer" feeling to simply the lack of any peer in the boat to discuss the issues in her life. As she says, "As captain, I had to force myself to look forward, over the bow."[5] As the book unfolds, the reader starts to see that eventually she will have to come to grips with the challenges of her nomadic life on the deep ocean. It foreshadows her eventual decision, revealed at the end of the book, that she would leave the sword-fishing world and take on the more accommodating (although still very challenging) life in the world of inshore lobster fishing in her own boat.

She also discusses the environmental challenges that have come to the fore in the two decades since she wrote her book. The challenges Ian Urbina describes in *The Outlaw Ocean*, published in 2019, are just touched upon in *The Hungry Ocean*, and her tone is a tad defensive. She says, "US fisherman are not pirates. We are among the most regulated fishermen in the world, and the penalties for noncompliance are stiff. Fishermen of my generation are conservation-minded."[6] The comments seemed a bit ironic a few years later, when in 2009 she was convicted of illegally entering and illegally fishing in Canadian waters and was fined $38,000.

In the end, this is a book about command at sea. A deep love of the ocean and the peculiar and challenging craft of long-line swordfish hunting fill the pages of the book. The reader will find that captain Linda—often called "Ma" by her crew—has to make the hard decisions again and again. "Making unpopular decisions is part of being the captain." That is true for any boss in any profession, but the oceans are a particularly difficult setting for leadership skills. Linda Greenlaw is a fine sea captain, and her love of boats and the sea are at the heart of *The Hungry Ocean*.

Bonus: Obviously, Sebastian Junger's *The Perfect Storm* is a good companion. But so is Joseph Conrad's "The Secret Sharer" and, of course, Ian Urbina's *The Outlaw Ocean*.[7] The portrayal of Linda Greenlaw in the film version of *The Perfect Storm* is accurate and poignant, given the outcomes.

CHAPTER TEN

THE OUTLAW OCEAN
Journeys across the Last Untamed Frontier

by Ian Urbina

For all its breathtaking beauty, the ocean is also a
dystopian place, home to dark inhumanities.[1]

I will always remember the first time I entered the South China Sea. It is a big body of water, about the size of the Caribbean Sea and the Gulf of Mexico combined, and today is entirely claimed by China as territorial waters. But this was in the mid-1970s, and I was in my early twenties, a junior officer assigned to a Navy destroyer, USS *Hewitt*. We were headed south by southwest into the Taiwan Strait at the northern opening to the body of water. We were hugging the Taiwanese side of the strait, trying to avoid any confrontation with warships of the People's Liberation Army Navy.

I walked onto the bridge just before midnight on a moonless evening to assume the watch as officer of the deck. The heat and humidity of the tropical air hit me. I smelled wood smoke, gasoline, and fish. Glancing at the radar, I saw hundreds of contacts ahead of us—it was a myriad of fishing vessels, whether Chinese,

Taiwanese, Thai, or Vietnamese we didn't know. It was clear I was in for a long and dangerous night trying to slip through their fishing operations without a collision or entangling their nets in our propellers. Fortunately, the sea was glass-calm, and most of the boats were brightly lit.

We must have looked like a monster to them, an 8,000-ton warship with only our required running lights, gliding on gas turbine power through the quiet sea. For the most part, they tried to avoid us, and we them, but again and again we had to pass close aboard the relatively small craft. I'll never forget the fishermen, small and slight, wearing minimal clothes, and hauling on nets. Their faces would turn up briefly to register our steel dragon sailing by, then return with resignation to a brutally hard task. It took us a couple of hours to pick through the fleet, and our captain stayed on the bridge the whole time. He was a wise old sea dog, and as we cleared the fishing fleet around 2 a.m., he lit up a Marlboro on the bridge wing and looked back. "Poor bastards," he said, and flicked his cigarette into the South China Sea.

Over the long decades of my time at sea, I went on to sail through many fishing fleets and to see many crimes at sea: clear overfishing, the use of illegal nets, oil and air pollution at significant scale, contraband and arms smuggling, narcotics transport, oil theft, piracy, trash and plastics dumping, and—worst of all—refugees left to die by merchants before we came on the scene. Often, in the latter stages of my career, I would observe that the oceans were by definition the largest crime scene in the world. But until I read Ian Urbina's brilliant and tragic book *The Outlaw Oceans*, I did not fully put a human face on all the crime I'd seen and at times tried to combat. What makes Urbina's work so remarkable is the degree to which he humanizes both the crimes and the people trying to stop them, and the herculean efforts he made to write the book. He labored for forty months (eighteen of them while on leave of absence from his day job at the *New York Times*), traveled 251,000 miles, boarded eighty-five planes, visited forty cities and every continent, and sailed over 12,000 nautical miles across all five oceans and twenty other seas. There may be more blue water in this book than any other in this sailor's library.

Urbina has worked primarily on investigative stories for the *New York Times*, winning both a Pulitzer Prize and a George Polk Award. A graduate of

Georgetown and the University of Chicago, he also worked as a Fulbright Fellow in Cuba and has written for a significant number of other publications as well as the *Times*. His gift is storytelling, and in each chapter of the book we uncover a different crime and meet a new cast of characters. This is "I was there" journalism at its best, and you can almost feel the slippery deck of the fishing factories at sea, slick with blood and fish guts; hear the plaintive voices of the trafficked victims, both children, women, and young men, as they tell their tales in broken English; or feel the tension in the air as he is present during a near mutiny. Urbina says, "At night, the sea is more a place of sounds than sights, and walking around the lower decks, I felt like a blind man in a haunted house. Metal whined. Hallways rattled as if someone had poured a bucket of loose screws into the walls. Waves slamming our sides sounded like the relentless crashes of a demolition derby. It was as though we were inside a lumbering beast that was being attacked, and we slowly rolled, twisted, and groaned our way forward."[2]

As Urbina points out again and again, the problem in addressing at-sea crime is a lack of clear laws and, above all, enforcement mechanisms. The first challenge, of course, is that the vast majority of the seas, which cover 70 percent of the world's surface, are international waters. Norms for policing them are laid out (somewhat) in the United Nations Convention on the Law of the Sea (generally known as the Law of the Sea Treaty). Restrictions on many of the criminal behaviors are addressed in general terms. But there is no "global police force" or "illegal maritime activity navy" that can enforce them. And even when criminals are apprehended by coast guards or navies, it is difficult to bring them to trial. Does the jurisdiction come from the nationality of the perpetrator? Or the national flag flown by the vessel? Or the closest coastal state? Or a nation that has passed national laws against certain activities?

And of course the sheer size and scale of maritime activity makes policing it incredibly difficult. When I commanded the NATO mission against piracy off the east coast of Africa, I had six ships at my disposal to patrol an area the size of Texas. Trying to stop crime in Texas with six police cars would be hard, to say the least. There was a sense on my ships that once the bad guys "go dark"—that is, turn off their automatic identification system (a beacon that tracks merchant ships)—they are largely free to do as they please. "Big ocean, not much cops," a narco-trafficker once said to me. In *The Outlaw Ocean*, we see the worst of what happens at sea, far from the glittering cruise ships and the sleek hulled warships. Nearly 60 million people work on the oceans in fishing boats alone, according to Urbina, and nearly 2 million on board the freighters and tankers that haul 90 percent of the world's goods.[3] There is plenty of motive and opportunity for criminal acts, and this book lays out the most dangerous in vivid strokes.

This is a long, dense but incredibly readable book. The reader will think again and again: "Can that really be happening?" Unfortunately, I can assure you it is, although even after nearly forty years in the U.S. Navy I learned things in *The Outlaw Ocean* that opened my eyes anew—and not in good ways.

Bonus: Try the novel *Polar Star* by Martin Cruz Smith. Set on a Soviet-era fish factory ship, it brings a personal backstory to some of the vignettes in *The Outlaw Ocean*. The book also has the wonderful fictional detective Arkady Renko (from *Gorky Park* and other Martin Cruz Smith novels) improbably at sea.

CHAPTER ELEVEN

THE SEA AROUND US

by Rachel L. Carson

On land and sea, the stream of life poured on. New forms evolved; some old ones declined and disappeared.[1]

R achel Carson was a brilliant writer and a fine scientist. She bridged those two worlds perfectly, writing a series of best-selling and highly regarded books about nature, including *Silent Spring*, which is widely regarded as a classic of environmental science that was published far ahead of its time. *The Sea around Us* is part of a trilogy of works she published, and it truly launched her into the eye of the public. It won both the 1952 National Book Award and several other prestigious prizes. Although she died prematurely in her mid-fifties, she lived a vitally important life as a conservationist before that term was widely appreciated.

Originally a marine biologist, she was working in the U.S. government before embarking on a career as an independent researcher and writer, and she always had a deep, instinctive feel for the ocean that comes through in her lyrical writing. I've read many, many books that try to describe the power and glory of the deep ocean, but none eclipses the writing of Rachel Carson. Grounded as a scientist, studying at both Johns Hopkins and Woods Hole Oceanographic Institution, she also taught for several years at the undergraduate level. One biographic statement says of Carson, "she made the sea her laboratory."[2] She was also an accomplished diver and small-boat mariner. In preparing to write *The Sea around Us*, Carson met with leading oceanographers who helped sharpen the content. But the gorgeous prose is all Rachel Carson and is what makes her books so extraordinary.

The Sea around Us is organized thematically (as opposed to chronologically, as many such volumes tend to be). This is probably because nine of the original chapters appeared as magazine articles in the *New Yorker* and *Nature* magazine, among other outlets. Part 1, consisting of eight chapters, is titled "Mother Sea." It includes material on the formation of the earth, the origins of the oceans, and the various periods of geological time stretching back to the pre-Cambrian periods over 500 million years ago. She addresses the surface of the oceans, the life cycle in the maritime world, and the "sunless sea" below the penetration of light. As she points out in the chapter on that deep ocean, it actually covers well over half the earth: "If we subtract the shallow areas of the continental shelves and the scattered banks and shoals, where at least the pale ghost of sunlight moves over the underlying bottom, there still remains about half the earth that is covered by miles-deep, lightless water, that has been dark since the world began."[3] It is a world where, to quote the poet Matthew Arnold, "great whales come sailing by/ sail and sail, with unshut eye."[4]

Carson also pays special attention to the earth's topography under the surface of the oceans in two chapters, "Hidden Lands" and "The Long Snowfall." The latter studies the movement of sediments from the land, carried by the rains into the sea. Perhaps the most moving chapter in the book is "The Birth of an Island," which—as the name suggests—takes the reader through the creation of islands around the world. She uses Bermuda as the frame of the conversation but touches on other isolated islands from the Galapagos to South Trinidad. In the final chapter of this first part, "The Shape of Ancient Seas," Carson focuses on the rising sea levels that have come to be such a crucial part of the global climate conversation today.

The second part of the book, "The Restless Sea," focuses more on the interaction of mankind and the oceans. Here her writing helps us understand the complex relationships of tide, wind, sun, and moon and how they have influenced global shipping, for example. In the second chapter of this part, "The Global Thermostat," she again is seventy years ahead of the climate conversation by focusing on the relationship of warming oceans to global warming—and its real and potential effects. As she correctly emphasizes, the connection between sea temperature and air temperature is crucial to the creation of weather. As she says, "the ocean dominates the air" and "evidence that the top of the world is growing warmer is to be found on every hand."[5] She closes the chapter with words that echo powerfully today: "But the long trend is toward a warmer earth; the pendulum is swinging."[6]

The final chapter of this short and powerful book, "The Encircling Sea," sweeps across the history of exploration from the ancient Greeks through the Vikings and on to the golden age of exploration when Magellan's expedition first circumnavigated the earth. Carson makes the point that, in the end, we are surrounded by the oceans. As the British say, "the sea is one," meaning it is connected everywhere, unlike the continents and islands of the earth.

There is no better way to close this brief snapshot of *The Sea around Us* than with Carson's words, written with the rolling pace of the deep ocean:

> For the sea lies all about us. The commerce of all lands must cross it. The very winds that move over the lands have been cradled on its broad expanse and seek ever to return to it. The continents themselves dissolve and pass to the sea in grain after grain of eroded land. So, the rains that rose from it return again in rivers. In its mysterious past it encompasses all the dim origins of life and receives in the end, after, it may be, many transmutations, the dead husks of that same life. For all at last return to the sea—to Oceanus, the ocean river, like the ever-flowing stream of time, the beginning and the end.[7]

Alpha and omega indeed. Rachel Carson's unique and powerful voices stretches on to our times today and will remain with sailors for all the ages to come.

CHAPTER TWELVE

THE WORLD IS BLUE
How Our Fate and the Ocean's Are One

by Sylvia A. Earle

If there is one thing most of us know about
the ocean, it's that it's big.

—Bill McKibben, American environmentalist[1]

This sensible and comprehensible volume, published in 2009, is in many ways a follow-on to the more lyrical but less scientific book by Rachel Carson, *The Sea around Us*. Sylvia Earle was once called "her deepness" by *The New Yorker*, and, indeed, the depth of her knowledge (pun intended) is on full display here. She has been a National Geographic explorer-in-residence since the late 1980s and was named a "Hero of the Planet" by *Time* magazine. Within government, she served as chief scientist for the U.S. National Oceanic and Atmospheric Administration (NOAA). A native of coastal Florida, she holds a BS from Florida State as well as an MS and a PhD from Duke University in phycology (the study of algae). She has had a long and adventurous life and won a slew of prizes, all for her study of the oceans from a scientific standpoint. She is also an expert diver and an accomplished small-boat handler.

Of note, she was among the first female "aquanauts" and has spent thousands of hours of her life underwater. Alongside her husband, Graham Hawkes, she was involved in building the research submersible *Deep Rover*, which operates to a depth of well over three thousand feet. During her tenure at NOAA as chief scientist, she focused on oil spills and their impact on the sea, leading to several trips to the Middle East to examine damage off the coast of Iraq. This led to her expertise being applied in the wake of the massive *Deepwater Horizon* disaster in the Gulf Coast. There is no living American with a deeper (that pun again) knowledge of the oceans, and her credentials as a mariner are exceptional.

In *The World Is Blue*, she lays out a persuasive and well-written case that the 70 percent of the earth that is water is the defining characteristic of our voyage on this planet. Much as *Silent Spring* by Rachel Carson energized global environmentalism on behalf of reducing pesticides and respecting the planet, Sylvia Earle shows us how the destructive behavior of the past half century is leading us down a potentially apocalyptic course. Her particular expertise is in the connections in the vast maritime ecosystem, and in demonstrating that the era of an "inexhaustible ocean" is over. Her research and many personal anecdotes cover a broad range of dangerous ocean activities, including overfishing and extinction of thousands of species of ocean-dwelling plants, mammals, and fish; vast pollution, especially the dumping of plastics and toxic materials (including radioactive); and the still-growing damage that will inevitably follow global warming and rising ocean temperatures.

One marker upon which she rightfully focuses is the rapidly accelerating death of coral reefs resulting from changes in ocean chemistry and temperature. Her research suggests that well over half of earth's coral reefs are dying or dead—a staggering number. This is exacerbated by the rise of so-called dead zones, wherein the loss of ocean oxygen is creating deserts at sea. In the Pacific Ocean, there is a field of floating plastics nearly the size of the state of Texas, and more damage will follow unless we reverse course. The book is beautifully illustrated with black-and-white photos that illuminate the real costs: tropical fish, seals, eels, octopi, clams, sea stars, sponges, and even fungi are all on display in their natural habitat. As she eloquently points out, we are in danger of "unraveling the fabric of life in the sea" if we break the complex chains of biodiversity.

One of the most powerful chapters—based on her own deep experience (can't help myself) is titled "Drilling, Mining, Shipping, Spilling," four words that should strike fear in the heart of any mariner or landsman who loves the sea and understands how we depend on it. The chapter opens with a full-page photo of the post-conflict fires burning in Kuwait in 1991 and moves on to an in-depth analysis of the stalled attempts to conduct "deep seabed mining" to recover nodules supposedly full of manganese, cobalt, copper, and nickel. The chapter then discusses the real heart of ocean exploitation: oil and gas recovery. Earle captures the big economic incentives but lays out a reasonable action plan to deal with them and avoid further damage to the offshore (and, increasingly, deep-water) environments. In the decade since she published the book, such exploitation has only accelerated, especially in the contested waters of the Eastern Mediterranean and the tense South China Sea. As she points out, the further melting of Arctic ice will only increase competition in the high north as more deposits become accessible.

The real heart of the book is the chapter "Changing Climate, Changing Chemistry." At the dark end of the spectrum, further damage over time may retard photosynthesis in the sea, leading to diminished oxygen supplies for the planet. Her descriptions of scientific research (you can't control what you can't measure) are the crucial first step in solving the challenges ahead. She addresses the all-important "what to do" question in the final third of the book, a call to action with the very direct title of "Now Is the Time: Opportunities for Action." Whether you are a seasoned mariner with years of seagoing experience or a landsman who simply loves and respects the oceans, this chapter lays out concrete ways in which all of us can impact the future of the oceans and, therefore, the planet. She talks about everything from smart aquaculture to creating protected marine sites around the world, and this section—like the entire book—is readable and compelling. The final section is the text of a TED Talk she gave in 2009, which is worth the price of the book, and worth watching online. In it she says, "If you think the ocean isn't important, imagine Earth without it. Mars comes to mind. No ocean, no life-support system." Her deepness gets it dead right. This is a powerful, practical, and moving book for *The Sailor's Bookshelf*.

CHAPTER THIRTEEN

WATCH OFFICER'S GUIDE, 16TH EDITION

by Adm. James Stavridis, USN (Ret.), Rear Adm. Robert P. Girrier, USN (Ret.), Capt. Tom Ogden, USN, and Capt. Jeff Heames, USN

The sea is eternally demanding, presenting myriad challenges
to the watch stander: ship handling, weather, the rules of the nautical
road, engineering, formation and convoy steaming, communications,
navigation, and under way safety, to name just a few.[1]

This compact volume first appeared in 1911 and has now gone through sixteen subsequent editions. I have personally edited or coedited the last three of these editions, each time working with many fellow mariners to make sure the material contained within the covers of this taut handbook of the naval profession is thorough, well presented, and completely up to date. Every time I walk on board a Navy ship, I make my way to the bridge, and there I will inevitably find a copy of *Watch Officer's Guide*. I cannot count the number of volumes I have signed over the years, a fact I mention not in self-aggrandizement but rather to point out that across my decades of engagement with this classic, several generations of bridge watchstanders have sailed uncounted sea miles.

What makes this book special, even for a landsman, is that it presents a very succinct view of how a naval officer is trained and prepared to assume the watch on a ship at sea. An old-fashioned nautical term is "forehandedness," loosely meaning being ready for anything by thinking ahead. As a ship's captain, I would constantly tell my bridge watchstanders to "think ahead of the problem" and to be "forehanded." They may have gotten tired of Cap'n Stavridis for pounding that into their psyche, but I believe we avoided many a problem by focusing on it, including a few collisions, damage due to heavy weather, and perhaps even a man overboard or two.

A good way to think about this idea of being forehanded as a watchstander is a quote from Adm. Ernest King, a tough, salty old Navy admiral who led the Navy through World War II. He was so famously difficult to deal with that his own daughter said of him, "He shaves with a blowtorch." Admiral King, who did not suffer fools lightly, to say the least, would often point out that "the secret of great shiphandling is never getting in a situation that requires great shiphandling." Amen to that, and *Watch Officer's Guide* is designed first and foremost to allow an apprentice or even an experienced mariner to think about the challenges that could emerge across a wide variety of danger zones.

The book is also quite good for the lay reader who simply wants to know what it is like to be on the bridge of a U.S. Navy warship. And, frankly, the basics of watchstanding apply not only to our Navy but to the Coast Guard, merchant marine, allied navies (much of the lore in the book, by the way, can be traced to the British Royal Navy), and even on the bridges of warships run by the oddly named People's Liberation Army Navy, or PLAN, of China. It begins simply with a general set of observations about taking over the watch on the bridge as the officer of the deck (OOD). The book covers the relationship of the OOD with the engineering officer of the watch (EOOW) down in the engineering plant; the combat information center officer (CICO), who is the bridge watch officer's backup in the CIC; and the authority of the captain, the navigator, and the senior watch officer. There is a useful discussion of the qualities of a good bridge watchstander: forehandedness, vigilance, judgment, intuition, experience, leadership, and a high level of energy are all critical.

Subsequent chapters get down to the specifics of standing a competent watch. There is a fairly detailed discussion of how to handle the ship; safely navigate the vessel; use the right set of so-called standard commands (essentially providing directions to the sailors actually driving the ship with a helm and speed controls); more detail on the engineering plant and the OOD role in its safe operation; and a summary of the international "rules of the road," which are the traffic safety requirements that every OOD (military or civilian) must have at his or her fingertips. A bridge watchstander must, of course, have a good knowledge of weather and its impact on operations as well as very detailed knowledge of how to operate the ship's boats and aircraft.

Watch Officer's Guide concludes with a very valuable set of checklists for the conduct of operations. A word of explanation here: while landsmen may think of naval operations as quite dashing and at times conducted with intuition, they are in fact very precisely orchestrated. Every good warship (and most civilian vessels) have detailed checklists—often laminated to keep track of events with a grease pencil and ensure everything is moving along smoothly and smartly. The checklists include "standing orders" (direction the captain provides to the OOD to execute operations in the captain's absence), schedule for both getting under way and entering port, lists for operating in poor visibility, a list for towing or being towed (hopefully not necessary), air operations for ships with either helicopter or fixed wing, and pollution-control measures. A good watchstander is constantly pulling out one of these comprehensive checklists to make sure the entire team is working together.

As I write in the preface to this sixteenth edition, these are challenging duties, not learned in a day, or exclusively by reading books like *Watch Officer's Guide*. Honing these skills requires study, to be sure, but also real deckplate experience, review, and education. It is worth pointing out that many of the skills of a good bridge watchstander are the same skills that can help anyone on the voyage of life—a calm outlook, steady hand at the wheel of your career, a perspective gained from looking at the far horizon, and that ineffable quality of forehandedness—that is, being prepared for whatever squall appears on your course. Dipping from time to time into *Watch Officer's Guide* can help steady anyone, on the sea or ashore.

EXPLORERS

CHAPTER FOURTEEN

ACROSS THE TOP OF THE WORLD
The Quest for the Northwest Passage

by James P. Delgado

I, too, would suffer in a cause—not in the blazing desert on
the way to Jerusalem, but in the frozen North on the way
to new knowledge in the unpierced unknown.

—Roald Engelbregt Gravning Amundsen, Norwegian explorer[1]

W hat do the shipwrecks of the luxury liner RMS *Titanic*; USS *Independence*, a World War II aircraft carrier; the civil war heavy gunboat USS *Monitor*; the battleships USS *Arizona* and USS *Nevada*; the slave ship *Clotilda*; and the lost treasure fleet of Kublai Khan all have in common? They were explored—along with a hundred other shipwrecks—by marine archaeologist and veteran diver James Delgado. He is a Fellow of the Royal Geographical Society, the internationally recognized Explorer's Club, and the

Royal Canadian Geographical Society. Armed with a PhD in archaeology and deep experience at sea, he became the first maritime historian of the National Park Service in 1987. Over the past several decades he has also been involved in many television presentations and published thirty-three books. Given his extensive diving and archaeological background as well as his ability to write and present so fluently, he is as close as the United States has come to producing a modern-day Jacques Cousteau (absent the flair for invention and the marine biology bent).[2]

Having delved into many of Dr. Delgado's books and viewed several of his captivating presentations online, I found this particular work, *Across the Top of the World*, among the very best. First and foremost, it is exceptionally well written, capturing the reader from the first few pages, detailing the history of the search for the Northwest Passage, a sea route sailing the Atlantic Ocean across the top of our home continent in North America and coming eventually to the Pacific Ocean and its rich trading opportunities. A second reason the book has landed on *The Sailor's Bookshelf* is that it captures so well the mariner's fascination with the unknown portions of the sea. From the first voyages in the mid-1500s to the eventual success of Roald Amundsen at the beginning of the twentieth century, Delgado lays out an obsessive quest that cost many, many lives and much treasure before it was finally completed. Finally, the book is printed on museum-quality paper, framed in an oversized edition, and spectacularly illustrated with photographs (many of them vintage and difficult to find elsewhere), well-drawn maps and charts, and moving works of art. The painting *The Last Voyage of Henry Hudson*, for example, showing the doomed explorer cast adrift by mutineers in a small boat in the early 1600s with a young boy (his son?) looking imploringly at him, is heartbreaking and beautiful.[3]

While the material covering the explorations covers roughly 450 years, Delgado arranges it both chronologically and geopolitically—covering the competition among the European nations as the centuries unfolded and explaining why the Northwest Passage was so highly valued. Logically enough, he opens the work with a beautifully illustrated precis of the environment of the Arctic, including the indigenous people, broadly known as the Inuit. As in *Moby-Dick*'s treatment of the whaling culture, Delgado does a highly credible job exploring the technology of the Inuit, from kayaks to heavy clothing, that would have greatly helped the Europeans if they had adopted it. He then moves on to the English explorer Martin Frobisher, an "Elizabethan seadog" willing to take extreme risk in return for a potential high reward. A contemporary of Sir Francis Drake and a favorite of Queen Elizabeth I, Frobisher failed in the quest for the passage and shifted his sights to raiding for Spanish gold. Another Englishman, Henry Hudson, found the great Canadian bay that bears his name but also failed to achieve a passage and eventually paid with his life following a mutiny on his fourth voyage. Other voyages and explorers followed (including, notably, Englishmen Edward Parry and John Franklin), but still the passage remained elusive into the early 1800s. Delgado brilliantly weaves into the narrative the reactions and recollections of the Inuit, who watch this parade of Europeans come and go, decade after decade.

By mid-1800s John Franklin—then fifty-nine, an old man by the norms of the day—is given yet another crack at the mission, setting out in 1845. The two ships of his expedition, *Terror* and *Erebus*, simply disappeared and by 1848 a rescue mission was sent after them. Eventually traces of the doomed expedition were discovered, all of the effort having been spurred on by the forceful and resourceful wife of John Franklin, Jane Griffin, Lady Franklin. Indeed, the central narrative in *Across the Top of the World* is the story of Sir John, and Delgado tells the long tale well.

A new generation of Arctic explorers emerged in the late nineteenth and early twentieth centuries, including the intrepid Norwegian Roald Amundsen, who looms large in both Arctic and Antarctic exploration. Amundsen took a different approach, using Inuit "technology" from sled dogs to animal skins, and a very small, shallow draft boat, the *Gjoa*. The story of his 1903 voyage through the Northwest Passage is in many ways the culmination of this fine book.

I have sailed the waters of the high north, and—as Supreme Allied Commander at NATO some years ago—focused on the challenges of the Arctic region in depth. It remains unique among the world's largest sea regions for having (thus far) avoided the kind of all-out wars we have seen virtually everywhere else (excepting its counterpart in the south, Antarctica). It is also unique for the grave difficulty of operating effectively north of the Arctic Circle. That is changing somewhat as global warming causes melting ice, and the Northwest Passage over which the European explorers contended so vigorously for nearly half a millennium is rapidly become a simple reality and quite navigable for more and more of the year. The Canadian military used to say, "high north, low tension," but each passing year seems to add real competition from Russia on one side and the five NATO Arctic nations (United States; Canada; Denmark, because of Greenland, which they own; Iceland; and Norway) on the other. China is increasingly interested in the strategic minerals, oil, and gas of the region as well as the opening trade routes. All of this means that even as the Northwest Passage becomes so much more accessible, it is potentially going to become mired in geopolitics. All the more reason that a volume like Dr. Delgado's should be required reading for sailors and landsmen alike as they seek to understand the heritage of Arctic exploration and therefore the context of today's challenges in the high north.

Bonus: There is a fulsome discussion of the issues in the high north today in my earlier book, *Sea Power: The History and Geopolitics of the World's Oceans* in the chapter on the Arctic.[4] It provides a contemporary view of the tensions and challenges in this distant part of the earth.

CHAPTER FIFTEEN

BLUE LATITUDES
Boldly Going Where Captain Cook Has Gone Before

by Tony Horwitz

Cook not only redrew the map of the world, creating a picture of the globe much like the one we know today; he also transformed the West's image of nature and man.[1]

W hen I was a brand-new ensign in the Navy, my first job was antisubmarine warfare officer on a recently commissioned *Spruance*-class destroyer of around 8,000 tons, USS *Hewitt*. I had just graduated from Annapolis and gone through six months of various additional schooling before reporting to the ship in my dream home port of San Diego, California. I arrived at the ship on a Monday, and just a few weeks later we headed west into the deep Pacific for a six-month forward deployment. This was at a time when the

Persian Gulf was considered a sleepy little spot visited by few U.S. Navy warships, as opposed to today when nearly all the West Coast deployments head there. In the mid-1970s, the Cold War was raging, China was still a sleeping giant, and our mission was to "show the flag" across the Pacific Ocean. My destroyer was part of the small three-ship flotilla, along with another destroyer, which was a sister ship of the *Spruance* class, and a medium-sized logistic ship to keep us supplied with fuel, food, and repair parts. The logistic ship was the USS *Niagara Falls*, a combat stores ship of about 20,000 tons. Our cruising itinerary was a sailor's dream: first Hawaii for a few days, then south across the equator to Fiji, on to Tonga and New Zealand. We did several days in each port, including two separate port visits in Kiwiland. Up next was Sydney, then up the east coast of Australia to Townsville by the Great Barrier Reef and thence up north to Darwin. For the next few months, we continued all around the Pacific, calling in the Philippines, Singapore, South Korea, Hong Kong, Japan, and several Micronesian islands including Guam. All told, we sailed close to 50,000 nautical miles in six months.

All through the cruise, I felt the ghost of Capt. James Cook, arguably the greatest explorer in history, at my back. His voyages through the Pacific echo down to the present day, and his story is above all a sailor's tale. Thus, he lands on *The Sailor's Bookshelf* with not one but two books: a superb biography, *Captain Cook: Master of the Seas* by Frank McLynn and the subject of this review, the wryly named *Blue Latitudes: Boldly Going Where Captain Cook Has Gone Before*. Of all the somewhat paired books on the list, these two deserve to be read in tandem. I will leave a summary of Cook's quite extraordinary life to the review of McLynn's fine volume, and instead I shall concentrate here on Tony Horwitz's approach.

First, I want to say I've loved Tony Horwitz's books over the years. He was an outstanding reporter at the *Wall Street Journal* who won the Pulitzer Prize for national reporting in the mid-1990s for a series on work in low-paying jobs across the country. His books are an eclectic mix, including two with a particular focus on the American Civil War: *Confederates in the Attic: Dispatches from the Unfinished Civil War* and *Midnight Rising: John Brown and the Raid that Sparked the Civil War*. As I was preparing *The Sailor's Bookshelf*, I knew I wanted to include his *Blue Latitudes* and was saddened to learn he had collapsed and died while walking through Washington, D.C., in the spring of 2019 at the age of sixty. His was a vital and meaningful voice, and he was in the middle of promoting a new book (his tenth) when he passed. I had briefly met him at a D.C. book-signing, and he crackled with intelligence and energy, that best of all combinations. Sail proud, Tony.

The thesis of *Blue Latitudes* is simple to state and hard to execute: travel as much of Captain Cook's voyages as possible (Cook made three epic cruises in the mid-1700s) and report on how the story has turned out in the intervening 250 years. How did New Zealand develop? How about Tonga? Tahiti? What about Alaska, Hawaii, and the appropriately named Savage Island? It is an audacious idea, and Horwitz brings it off brilliantly, writing anecdotally about the present day but constantly bringing the reader back to the touchstone of Cook himself. Indeed, just the scale of Cook's exploration is hard to comprehend. When James Cook left London for the Pacific in 1768, perhaps a third of the world globe was essentially terra incognita—an unknown blank on charts and maps. By the time Cook died in an unnecessary fight ashore with locals in the Hawaiian islands in 1779, the mapping was essentially finished. His voyages took him north to the Arctic and south to the great continent of Antarctica as well as from Indonesia at the gateway to the eastern Pacific to the shores of western South America. For Horwitz to undertake a modern recreation of Cook's journeys is a breath-taking idea, and he tells the story beautifully.

He begins in a sense at the end of the tale, with the moment that the remains of the murdered Captain Cook are returned to his ship, *Resolution*, by the Hawaiians. (Interestingly, the young and brilliant but mercurial master of that vessel is William Bligh). Horwitz then starts his journey by sailing in a replica of Cook's earlier ship, *Endeavour*. Along with a small professional crew and about forty volunteers, the ship sails along part of the route Cook sailed, rotating the volunteers from port to port. The construct of *Blue Latitudes* is simple: each chapter begins with a set piece from the voyages of Cook, then shifts to the present day in the same locale. Thus, we see both Cook and our modern-day selves at the edge of the sea around the vast Pacific: Tahiti, Bora Bora, New Zealand, the Great Barrier Reef, Savage Island, Tonga, Alaska, and ultimately to Hawaii, where Cook meets his fate. The book is full of easily readable maps, and the historical rendering is impeccable, based almost entirely on Cook's own logs and contemporary first-person accounts.

My own copy of this remarkable book, by the way, is stamped with the logo of USS *Enterprise*, the nuclear-powered aircraft carrier then under my command as part of a carrier strike group in combat in 2002–4. I find that stamp from *Enterprise* slightly ironic, given the echoes of Cook's voyages that permeate the "voyages of the starship *Enterprise*" under not James Cook but James Kirk. As Tony Horwitz points out, James Cook—James Kirk; *Endeavour*—*Enterprise*; and both of them quite literally going where "no [European] man has gone before."

This is a creative and wonderfully realized book about how the vast Pacific contains and shapes so many places and cultures, and the conceit of matching Cook's first glimpse, balanced with how the story has turned out thus far, makes for a fine voyage for any sailor or landsman alike.

Bonus: *Captain Cook: Master of the Seas* by Frank McLynn should be read alongside this. For a more ambitious dive, of course, the actual journals of Captain Cook (1768–79) are widely available and highly readable. Horwitz refers to them constantly and weaves them into his storytelling seamlessly.

CHAPTER SIXTEEN

CAPTAIN COOK
Master of the Seas

by Frank McLynn

From now on [after combat in the
Seven Years' War] the real enemy would always
be the cruel, implacable ocean.[1]

G enerally, I dislike sports analogies, but the sporting term "GOAT" (great-est of all time) really applies to Capt. James Cook. He was the leader in almost every category of exploration, including total miles sailed, number of specific discoveries, creation of new maps and charts, and a dozen other metrics. In writing about *Blue Latitudes*, I tell of my own Pacific cruises as an ensign, which had a hint of Cook-like span of geography. But unlike Captain Cook, I had indoor plumbing, excellent food, an 8,000-ton ship under my feet, high-end communications reaching any point on earth, and precise celestial and electronic navigation. I would blush to compare even my entire career—with over nine years spent at sea on the deep ocean when counted up, day for day—with the maritime experience of James Cook.

Of the many, many Cook biographies available, I prefer this one by Frank McLynn. A very well-educated scholar and professor of history, he became a full-time writer relatively early in his long career and has published more than twenty-five books, almost all biographies. I've only read two others besides the present volume, but both of those (biographies of the explorer Sir Richard Francis Burton and of Napoleon) are superb. Among many others, he has also written about Richard the Lionhearted, Pancho Villa, Robert Louis Stevenson, Carl Jung, and—most recently—Genghis Khan. His quintessential skill is putting the story of an individual into the larger context of the age, and in the case of James Cook that ability is on full display. He contextualizes Cook as representing the age of exploration and particularly an expression of the expansion of British sea power as that country moved through the 1700s to become the Victorian Empire upon which the sun never sets (according to some French observers, this was because God did not trust the British in the dark). He also is blunt in describing the increasing brutality and flogging employed toward the end of the voyages (both of crewmembers and local people) that stain Cook's legacy.

Born in the north of England in 1728, Cook had only five years of formal education and was essentially self-taught in almost all things. After a few months apprenticed in a shop, he became a merchant sailor, initially working coastal small ships and learning the mathematic skills he would eventually need for celestial navigation and charting. By 1755 Cook had joined the Royal Navy, descending again to the bottom of the maritime career ladder but then working himself upward. Cook's initial tours as a member of the Royal Navy included combat in the Seven Years' War, the precursor conflict to the Napoleonic era of near-constant combat that emerged by the end of the 1700s. He spent some years sailing off Canada, honing his navigational and hydrographic skills. Cook became determined to undertake major voyages of exploration, saying he wanted to go not only "farther than any man has been before me, but as far as I think it is possible for a man to go."[2]

He made three voyages, all under commission of the Admiralty for the purposes of science. The first began in 1768 on board HMS *Endeavour* and included significant discoveries and mapping around Tahiti and many other Polynesian islands before reaching the southeast coast of Australia in the spring of 1770. This was the first European arrival on that coast, and he made important botanical (naming Botany Bay) and anthropological discoveries. The cruise was viewed as an immense success in England, and Cook's fame and fortune after his return in 1771 rose. A second voyage, 1772–75, followed Cook's promotion to the rank of commander. This mission focused on the circumnavigation of New Zealand and included the ships HMS *Resolution* and HMS *Adventure*. On this voyage he went as far south as the Antarctic Circle. As McLynn says, "The three exploratory forays into the Antarctic Ocean during the second voyage together probably constitute Cook's greatest feat of discovery and navigation."[3] While headed back to England, he planted the British flag on South Georgia island, using for navigation a copy of John Harrison's H4 marine chronometer (see Dava Sobel's *Longitude* for the full story). After his return, he was made post-captain and a Fellow of the Royal Society.

By 1776, in his late forties, Cook was desperate to return to the sea and embarked on a third voyage, which continued until his untimely death in 1779. On this third trip, he discovered Hawaii and began a systematic exploration and mapping of the West Coast of North America. He continued northward through the Bering Sea, completing significant observations within the Arctic Circle in 1778 until he was blocked by sea ice. Cook returned to Hawaii and unfortunately entered into a series of confrontations with the native people of the big island. After the theft of one of Cook's small cutters, he went ashore to try to resolve the problems. As events unfolded on the beach, he was attacked, clubbed, and stabbed, dying at the scene. The Hawaiians took his body away and his bones were ritualistically removed from his corpse. Some were returned to the expedition, which were buried at sea by his crew.

There is immense controversy as to the circumstances of Cook's death. McLynn says, "Was he killed because the Hawaiians considered him an impostor or false god? Or had Cook plunged into a psychotic interlude? Was his murder on the shoreline justifiable homicide? Or was the entire debacle a chapter of accidents, a series of events that could have turned out otherwise."[4] I am struck by the similarity in the fickle nature of the events and the outcome on that fateful beach with the way the sea itself can change in an instant from something welcoming to something deadly. Perhaps that unpredictability is what met James Cook on that Hawaiian beach, and in that moment he was unprepared to deal with it as well as he had handled many other crises.

A good description of Cook is provided by a shipmate on *Resolution*, who said he was modest, somewhat bashful, tall for the day (over six feet), and very plain in dress and appearance. In McLynn's book, he is described as "tall, handsome, dark brown complexion, with a large, head, nose, forehead and brown eyes" and that he "seemed in a world of his own . . . when a commander, would often sit at table with his officers without saying a word."[5] There are memorials to Captain Cook all around the world, including, most notably, in Hawaii, Australia, New Zealand, and of course in the United Kingdom. There are Cook Islands, a Cook Strait, a Cook Inlet, and even a Cook crater on the moon—as well as a Mount Cook on the border between the United States and Canada. And he deserves every memorial, in my view, despite all his flaws. He was a giant in the world of exploration and a gifted navigator, sea captain, and leader. As long as sailors ply their trade on the vast Pacific, James Cook will be well and truly remembered.

> **Bonus:** For a sense of how the story of Cook's discoveries eventually played out, try *Blue Latitudes: Boldly Going Where Captain Cook Has Gone Before* by Tony Horwitz, also a book on *The Sailor's Bookshelf*. Naturally, the best bonus would be to read the actual journals of Captain Cook's three voyages. Often packaged as "Captain Cook's Voyages, 1768–1779," there are many formats. I like the one produced by the Folio Society of London in 1997, which is available through online used book dealers for under $35—a bargain.

CHAPTER SEVENTEEN

KON-TIKI
Six Men Cross the Pacific on a Raft

by Thor Heyerdahl

For, if one has fed a shark directly by hand once,
it is no longer amusing.[1]

One of the highlights of my time as NATO Supreme Allied Commander was visiting the Kon-Tiki Museum in Oslo, Norway. As the first admiral to take command of Alliance operations, I was a change from the usual general, and the nations I visited were always eager to show me their nautical museums and ship displays. I always wondered where the generals had been taken—perhaps to weapons armories or tank factories. To each his or her own, I suppose. I loved the nautical visits, and many of them were impressive indeed, and of large and imposing ships: HMS *Victory* at Portsmouth, for example, or the massive Swedish Royal warship *Vasa*, which sank in twenty minutes on its maiden voyage. All were fascinating to me.

But the one vessel that literally took my breath away was the raft *Kon-Tiki*, built by Norwegian explorer, mariner, and adventurer Thor Heyerdahl. It had been constructed out of balsa wood and other indigenous materials in the Polynesian islands based on drawings of the Incan rafts handed down from the Spanish conquerors. The theory that Thor Heyerdahl set out to prove was that the ancient Polynesians were in fact the first settlers of South America, after voyaging thousands of miles across the Pacific Ocean. He named the raft *Kon-Tiki* in homage to an ancient Incan god. Heyerdahl was determined to build a large raft in the style and using the tools available to the Polynesians in pre-Columbian times, perhaps three thousand years ago. He funded the experiment with private money (mostly personal loans) and took a crew of six total, including himself. While he did take some modern tools on board for safety (such as a radio, sextant, watches, nautical charts, some bladed weapons), none of these were used to make the voyage succeed.

He set out in late spring of 1947, on April 28, and sailed for 101 days for some 4,300 nautical miles, launching from Peru and ending on a reef at Raroia in the Tuamotus islands on August 7. Happily, Thor Heyerdahl had a gift for writing and photography, and his book *Kon-Tiki* was published in 1948 in Norwegian and in English by 1950. The first edition I have in my hand today came out in September of that year, and I've read it several times over the years. The book is excellent, and so was the documentary Heyerdahl produced a year later, which won the Academy Award for best foreign-language film in 1951. The original raft, which I was privileged to see, is carefully preserved. It is a quite simple craft, of course, about fifty feet in length with a mangrove main mast of about thirty feet in height. Just behind the mast is a cabin made of bamboo that is about fifteen feet long and eight feet wide. *Kon-Tiki* has a steering oar of mangrove with a fir blade of around nineteen feet in length. There is not a shred of metal in the vessel.

On the voyage, the craft carried close to three hundred gallons of drinking water in a mix of modern (for safety) and ancient containers (to test the theory). The meals were simple: coconut, sweet potatoes, gourd squash, and other fruits and roots. Of note, the sailors were able to catch plenty of fish, including tuna, bonito, flying fish, mahi-mahi, and shark. One of the most amusing sections of the tale is the interactions with sharks, for which the crew managed to develop a fearless attitude, often pulling their tails and tempting them with bait put over the side by hand to get them to surface. The crew were all Norwegians, save one Swede and one parrot named Lorita. Sailing from the seaport of Callao on the coast of Peru, the *Kon-Tiki* made good time to an uninhabited Polynesian island in the Tuamotus, traveling about 1.5 nautical miles per hour—hardly a swift passage but sufficient to prove the possibility of east-to-west migration across the Pacific in the minds of some.

While most scientists continue to believe that the bulk of Polynesian settlement occurred with voyages (also very long and dangerous) from East Asia (i.e., west-to-east migration), there is still much unsettled anthropology and genetic science research that provides differing views. In a concluding note, Heyerdahl says, "My migration theory, as such, was not necessarily proved by the successful outcome of the *Kon-Tiki* expedition."[2] What is quite certain is that six brave men in a very primitive craft bonded deeply with the rolling Pacific Ocean. They came to love the small craft and for the rest of their days could each recall small details about their voyage. The *Kon-Tiki* was fairly smashed up on a reef while landing on the atoll but was towed out by a French ship and eventually rebuilt and placed on display in Oslo.

Thor Heyerdahl had a long and entertaining life, although his accomplishments on *Kon-Tiki* certainly stand out. He also sailed from the west coast of Africa to the Caribbean two decades after the *Kon-Tiki* voyage in another indigenous, local-material craft, the *Ra* and *Ra II*, named for the Egyptian sun god. While the first voyage was a failure, the second handily made the trip from Morocco to Barbados and is documented in both book and film. He built another boat, *Tigris*, trying to show a link between Mesopotamia and western India / eastern Pakistan. Heyerdahl took on numerous other archeological and anthropological projects, and he was never far from the sea in his work. He was married three times, had five children, and lived all over the world, dying in 2002 in his late eighties in Italy.

What I love about the book is simply the audacity of the voyage and the fascinating storytelling and visual descriptions. As *Kon-Tiki* was hauled on board a merchant ship in the Polynesian islands for the long voyage home, the crew stood on the deck near the craft. "Waves were breaking out in the blue sea. We could no longer reach down to them. White trade-wind clouds drifted across the blue sky. We were no longer traveling their way. We were defying Nature now. We were going back to the twentieth century which lay so far, far away."[3] For three glorious months, these Scandinavian mariners sailed back three thousand years. "The closer we came into contact with the sea and what had its home there, the less strange it became and the more at home we ourselves felt."[4] I envy their voyage, and including this story in *The Sailor's Bookshelf* honors their memory—as it does the ancient voyagers, whether they sailed from Asia or South America or both.

Bonus: The documentary *Kon-Tiki* won the Academy Award in 1951. It was directed by Thor Heyerdahl and is a perfect accompaniment to this. The novel *Pitcairn's Island*, the concluding volume in the *Mutiny on the Bounty* trilogy by James Norman Hall and Charles Nordhoff, is a portrait of Polynesian society, as in *Hawaii*, the 1959 novel by James Michener.

CHAPTER
EIGHTEEN

SAILING ALONE AROUND
THE WORLD

by Joshua Slocum

I grasped her gunwale and held on as she turned bottom
up, for I suddenly remembered that I could not swim.[1]

Time for a confession: I am *not* a skilled wind-driven sailor. While I would put my power-boat shiphandling skills up there with anyone's, I am not someone who can leap to the tiller or the wheel of a big (or small) sailing ship, glance up at the "telltales" on the sails, and masterfully bring the boat "closer to the wind." At Annapolis, every midshipman is given a basic course in sailing, and in the hot, humid summer of 1972 at age seventeen, I learned the theory and commands of how to handle a very small single-mast boat called a "knockabout." Good name, considering I managed to knock the 26-foot boat hard into the pier a couple of times trying to bring it back into dock on a breezy summer's day. The boats also had lead in their keels and were almost impossible to capsize.

I did a bit more sailing over the four years as part of training in seamanship and navigation, including some offshore sailing in the beautiful Naval Academy "yawls," decent-sized sailing boats of 44 feet in length, designed by famed naval architect Bill Luders. Sure, I love being up in the wind and out on a sailing boat on a beautiful day—who doesn't? And to this day, I jump at the chance to go out with a skilled captain. And I'm a card-carrying member of the New York Yacht Club. But my hosts on sailing boats are always disappointed to learn I'm not a skilled sailor. I'm a good crewman, happy to haul a line, rig a sail, and take a turn at the wheel—but a sailing captain, I emphatically am not. Give me four gas turbines, 100,000 shaft horsepower, twin screws and rudders, and I can nuzzle an 8,000-ton destroyer into a berth quite smoothly. As a result of my own inadequacy in pure sailing, I have deep respect for "real" sailors, who can read those maddening winds, rig just the right mix of sails, and tweak a course to pick up an extra knot or two.

One of the great pure sailors of all time was Joshua Slocum. Born in 1844 in eastern Canada (the "Maritimes," as my Canadian friends call them), he became an American citizen and one of the most renowned sailors of all time—deservedly, because he completed the first documented circumnavigation of the world alone in a sailboat. A severe-looking man in maturity with a completely bald head and a very full goatee, he grew up around and on the water, learning to sail from his earliest days. His grandfather was a lighthouse keeper, and his yearning for the sea and adventure led to several boyhood episodes of running away from home. Slocum's at-sea life really began when he was sixteen and signed onto a merchant ship headed for Europe. After knocking around at sea on several merchant ships, he took command for the first time in 1869 and sailed as a captain for the next several decades, often with his wife embarked. Indeed, his four children were born at sea on his ships. And his adventures literally around the world are too numerous to enumerate here. Suffice to say, this was a man "rocked in the cradle of the deep," with salt water in his veins.

Toward the turn of the century, in his early fifties, he decided to build a small sailing vessel and sail alone around the world. Essentially a rebuild, the gaff-rigged former oyster boat was called *Spray*, and in 1895 he wrote that he "resolved on a voyage around the world, and as the wind on the morning of April 24, 1895 was fair, at noon I weighed anchor, set sail, and filled away from Boston, where the *Spray* had been moored snugly all winter." It was the seminal moment in his life, and he'd describe it in this marvelous tale: "A thrilling pulse beat high in me. My step was light on deck in the crisp air. I felt there could be no turning back, and that I was engaging in an adventure the meaning of which I thoroughly understood."[2]

The book is a pure delight at every turn. It was published in 1900 and has remained in print for well over a century. I suspect it will never go out of print because it truly is a "first" in terms of the accomplishment but also because it is superbly written. Slocum was at sea from the spring of 1895 to the summer of 1898, initially crossing the Atlantic twice, navigating the Strait of Magellan, and crossing the Pacific. The final leg took him back for a third time across the Atlantic, and there were many stops along his 46,000-mile voyage, returning to Newport, Rhode Island, the unofficial capital of American sailing. Everywhere he went he was the toast of the waterfront, often giving talks and displaying photographs that were very well received. Along the way, he touched at many small islands, of course, and the list of stops reads a bit like Judith Schalansky's *Atlas of Remote Islands*, also on *The Sailor's Bookshelf*—the difference is that Joshua Slocum actually visited them all. In an echo of Joseph Conrad's "The Secret Sharer," he has an "imaginary crewmember" (who supposedly is a former sailor on the *Pinta* of Christopher Columbus's small flotilla).

Slocum faced all the perils one would expect: terrible weather, near collisions, piracy, sheer loneliness, mediocre food, near shipwreck, and plenty more. Joshua Slocum quite modestly makes *Spray* the real hero of the book, and by the end, the reader loves that little boat too. After some setbacks in later life (the price of fame), he again got under way in *Spray* hoping to reverse his fortunes with another voyage (and another book deal). After departing the United States in the early winter of 1909, he set sail for South America. He was never seen again, and his wife said she believed him lost at sea. Although he was not declared legally dead until 1924, his legacy as a sailing captain lives on to this day. And not only is his book still in print, the name *Spray* continues to grace the stern of many a sailing boat.

Bonus: Robert Stone's superb sailing novel, *Outerbridge Reach*, has echoes of Joshua Slocum throughout. It is the tale of a copywriter seeking an "around the world" sailing experience, which ends . . . ah, you should read the book.

CHAPTER NINETEEN

THE CONQUEST OF THE OCEAN
An Illustrated History of Seafaring

by Brian Lavery

The Ocean is the great unity.[1]

This is a stunningly illustrated volume that covers the entirety of mankind's relationship with the ocean across more than five thousand years of history. Brian Lavery, a former director of the British National Maritime Museum at Greenwich, is the highly regarded author of more than thirty-five books of naval history (he is by inclination a historian), leadership at sea, Nelson's navy, ships, sailing, and the seafaring life. I've met him on a couple of occasions, and he is also kind, thoughtful, and a fine storyteller. He did a star turn in the BBC documentary *Empire of the Seas* and was a consultant on the superb film version of Patrick O'Brian's novels, *Master and Commander: The Far Side of the World.* His book about the Royal Navy in the time of Lord Nelson is a masterpiece. Brian is also a skillful sailor with real hands-on experience at sea. I mention all of that to establish his true bona fides for publishing such a sweeping volume.

This is a very cleverly constructed and lavishly illustrated single volume that simply moves forward chronologically. It begins with the earliest voyages at sea by Polynesians navigating thousands of sea miles using only their knowledge of the sun, stars, wind, and currents. One of the dozens of maps in the book lays out these early voyages, and they are mind-boggling. Many of them occurred three thousand years before Christ strode into the Sea of Galilee to recruit the apostles, and individual voyages covered perhaps as much as fifteen hundred miles. Routes across the vast Pacific Ocean from East Asia to New Guinea, from Fiji to Samoa and on to Hawaii, from Tonga by the Cook Islands and on to Easter Island (see *Atlas of Remote Islands* by Judith Schalansky for a sense of these distances and the achievement to island-hop in this manner).

Also around 3,000 BCE, the mariners of the Eastern Mediterranean began to use primitive sails to propel themselves on short coastal voyages. Over time the Egyptians, Phoenicians, Greeks, and others combined sail and oars, and by 700 BCE (around the time Homer was writing *The Odyssey*) triremes and other hybrid warships emerged. At this point in the book Lavery begins to weave in the great sea battles of history, starting with the unlikely Greek triumph over invading Persians under Xerxes in 480 BCE at the Bay of Salamis near Athens. The Vikings next appear, including their voyages from Scandinavia by Iceland to Greenland, and on to North America to discover what they called "vineland"— which occurred hundreds of years before the voyages of Christopher Columbus.

I was particularly happy to see the treatment of Chinese admiral Zheng He in the book, as this intrepid explorer commanded vast fleets of perhaps a hundred ships and nearly 30,000 men in the early 1400s. He is featured in my book about character, *Sailing True North: Ten Admirals and the Voyage of Character* and is little known in much of the West. Yet his extraordinary voyages remain today perhaps the largest flotillas ever to operate together on the Indian Ocean, and they are the basis for the controversial claim by modern-day China for territorial rights over essentially the entire South China Sea.

An especially compelling section of the book concerns the "age of exploration," generally dated from 1450 to 1600. Herein are the stories of Columbus, of course, but also of Vasco da Gama and Bartolomeu Dias of the Portuguese court of Prince Henry the Navigator. We learn about the Portuguese caravels, highly maneuverable sailing ships; the Spanish carrack; the Venetian galley; and other new hull forms and sail configurations. By the early 1500s Ferdinand Magellan became the first to lead an expedition that circumnavigated the earth, although he personally did not survive the voyage. All of this gave significant power to Spain and Portugal, especially in creating huge colonial landholdings in the New World.

After the time of the global explorers, we learn how the seas become the enablers of new colonial empires that stretch around the world. From roughly 1600 through the mid-1800s, all of the major European states snatch up enormous tracts of distant lands and associated islands, turning most of them into economic engines and treasure bins to be stripped of slaves, gold, silver, minerals, and produce. During this time the "sun never sets on the British Empire" because of the Royal Navy and its ability to defend sea lanes of communication. The tragic story of slavery is laid out, again enabled by the conquest of the oceans. In this period perhaps the most consequential sea battle in British history occurs when Nelson defeats Napoleon's fleet at Trafalgar. This is a period in which Lavery is especially trenchant, and the illustrations and maps here are particularly good.

One of the best aspects of the book is its ability to weave the story of technological advancement at sea alongside the history and geopolitics. In the century stretching from the early 1800s to the early 1900s, the way in which sailors went to sea changed dramatically. From sail to coal to liquid fuel; from paddle wheelers and steamships to massive steel warships; from clipper ships and early submarines to the arrival of the huge luxury liners—all these stories are woven through this seminal period.

The final two major sections of the book deal, sadly, with a great deal of war. The major battles of the most recent century—Jutland, the Battle of the Atlantic, Midway, D-Day landings, the island campaign in the Pacific of World War II, the Cuban missile crisis, and the Falklands war. But he also discusses the exploration of the deep by Jacques Cousteau; the rise of America's Cup sailing, with many other ocean races; and the emergence of container ship trading. Appropriately, he closes with emerging concerns about the environment (with a snapshot of the *Exxon Valdez* disaster) and the growing lawlessness of the seas (see *The Outlaw Oceans* by Ian Urbina, also on *The Sailor's Bookshelf*).

Story piles on story, each told with verve and lots of historical detail. All of the illustrations and maps are first rate, and the sweep of the tale is truly magnificent. This is a book that a sailor or a landsman alike could reach for as a reference to a historical allusion, to check a style of sailing ship, or to learn a new story about Sir Francis Drake.

Bonus: A companion book, also by Brian Lavery, is *Nelson's Navy, Revised and Updated: The Ships, Men, and Organisation, 1793–1815.* This volume is an incredible deep dive into the British Royal Navy from the late 1700s to the early 1800s and is another masterpiece. To read and truly appreciate Patrick O'Brian's twenty-volume Aubrey-Maturin series, they must be read alongside *Nelson's Navy*.

CHAPTER TWENTY

THE ENDURANCE
Shackleton's Legendary Antarctic Expedition

by Caroline Alexander

It is beyond conception, even to us, that we are dwelling
on a colossal ice raft, with but five feet of ice separating us
from 2,000 fathoms of ocean and drifting along under the
caprices of wind and tides, to heaven knows where.

—Frank Hurley, expedition photographer[1]

I n 1999 I arrived at the Pentagon fresh from sea duty as a commodore of a
squadron of warships, including a cruiser, a frigate, and five destroyers—one
of them Canadian. It was a wonderful assignment at sea, including a forward
deployment with combat operations in the Arabian Gulf. I wasn't thrilled about
heading back to the Pentagon, but I had luckily been selected to be the executive
assistant (sort of a chief of staff) to Secretary of the Navy Richard Danzig, one
of the smartest persons I've ever spent a great deal of time around—a Rhodes
scholar, PhD in history, law degree from Yale, and possessor of an incredibly

74

successful career. Danzig and I bonded over a love of books, and our friendship continues to this day. And one of the initiatives he implemented was bringing into the office notable authors to give talks to the Secretary of the Navy staff.

The most impressive writer we had visit over my two years in that job was a woman named Caroline Alexander. She is British American and grew up in north Florida, where both my wife and I are from. She was among the first group of women to become Rhodes scholars and studied philosophy and theology at Oxford University. Caroline is also a world-class athlete, having competed in the national modern pentathlon for the United States. But her greatest gift is her pen. She has published a series of remarkable books and articles covering topics as diverse as butterfly poachers (who knew?), ancient history (she has translated the works of Homer), Xanadu, central Africa, and a host of other interesting and little-studied issues and locales. We invited her to the Pentagon to discuss her 1998 best-selling book *The Endurance: Shackleton's Legendary Antarctic Expedition*, about one of the most inspirational expeditions in the long history of exploration.

The book is a tour de force in telling the story of Sir Ernest Shackleton, who in the days just before World War I, set out with a crew of twenty-seven and sailed south through the deep Atlantic to Antarctica. His goal was to cross the great southern continent by foot. They sailed through the freezing Weddell Sea and were about one hundred miles from their goal when their three-mast barquentine sailing ship, *Endurance*, became trapped in the ice pack and eventually was crushed. This was the start of a true experience of "endurance," which would last twenty months before every member of the crew was rescued alive. They spent months in crude campsites drifting north on ice floes before taking to the remaining lifeboats and setting up another camp on Elephant Island in the South Shetland Islands. At this point, realizing the situation was truly dire, Shackleton and hand-picked members of his crew made an astounding eight-hundred-mile voyage in an open boat—the *James Caird*—to reach the island of South Georgia. Shackleton was then able to organize the rescue of the rest of his crew.

Caroline Alexander's book is wonderful, both for the writing and for the vintage photographs by Frank Hurley. It begins with an overview of the age of polar exploration, both successes and failures. It is a classic story of men heading to sea in the pursuit of great goals in the unexplored world beyond the reach of charts or maps. Shackleton emerges as a quintessential inspirational servant leader—his reputation was always one of deep concern about the sailors under his command. And his skilled seamanship was demonstrated again and again. As he brought the *James Caird* close to South Georgia and salvation, all seemed lost again as the small boat appeared poised to crash on a dreaded lee shore. He wrote: "I think most of us had a feeling that the end was very near."[2] But suddenly the wind veered yet again, and he was able to come about and save the boat. After seventeen days and fighting through a hurricane, they were ashore safely, having rescued themselves through the leadership of Shackleton against everything the sea could throw at them. It is without question one of the great sea boat voyages in history, and Alexander tells the story brilliantly.

Shackleton always kept hope alive for his crew, stood as a personal example in adversity, maintained a sense of humor, thought creatively about solutions to the worst problems, and kept his men at the task. That is the kind of captain to have, and Caroline Alexander—teaming with the incredible period photos of Frank Hurley—brings his legacy to life. When I went on to command a strike group, I gave many of the captains under my leadership a copy of this extraordinary book of survival, resilience, and the sea. I've often pulled it open to refresh myself (including when my wife and I went to Antarctica under much nicer circumstances in 2014). I have my signed copy by Caroline Alexander, and I treasure the story and honor the memory of Sir Ernest Shackleton.

Bonus: The flip side of the *Endurance* expedition was a tragic effort by Robert Falcon Scott in *Terra Nova*, setting out in 1910 to try to reach the South Pole. All died, and the book *The Birthday Boys: A Novel* by Beryl Bainbridge is a superb retelling of the sobering yet remarkable and tragic tale.

CHAPTER
TWENTY-ONE

THE SILENT WORLD
A Story of Undersea Discovery and Adventure, by the First Men to Swim at Record Depths with the Freedom of Fish

by Jacques-Yves Cousteau with Frédéric Dumas

The sea, once it casts its spell, holds one in
its net of wonder forever.[1]

I t is hard to overstate the impact on ocean awareness that a skinny, short French naval officer named Jacques-Yves Cousteau created during his long and highly public life. Born in 1910, Cousteau started spearfishing and snorkel-diving in the 1930s and always seemed most at ease in the water. He has said that "from birth, man carries the weight of gravity on his shoulders. He is bolted to earth. But man has only to sink beneath the surface and he is free."[2] In the 1940s he began experimenting with what was called "Aqua-Lung diving," using various apparatuses he invented and manufactured with a small coterie of colleagues, including his coauthor on this volume, Frédéric Dumas. Between the two of them, they probably accomplished well over 10,000 descents in a wide variety of scenarios, chiefly as what has come to be known in English as "scuba diving."

Not a formally trained scientist or marine biologist, Cousteau is more accurately thought of as a self-taught naturalist, inventor, author, and filmmaker. Cousteau spent several years in the United States as a child and spoke excellent English. He began his professional career as a naval officer and always self-identified as such. After attending the École Navale (the naval academy of France), he served as a gunnery officer in a vintage French battleship, *Condorcet*. While stationed in Toulon on the Mediterranean coast, he started to experiment with underwater equipment, including goggles and eventually primitive versions of the Aqua-Lung. By the late 1940s he was running a French navy undersea research group and commanding its research ship on expeditions. After departing the French navy in 1949, he went on in 1951 to take command of the now world-famous research vessel and floating laboratory *Calypso*, which became the center of his life and work for several decades.[3]

His international fame exploded with the publication of *The Silent World* in 1953. The book is part memoir, part photo essay, and part ecological policy advocacy. He begins by describing in detail the process of developing the Aqua-Lung and then unfolds the various adventures and cruises of *Calypso*. These include a search for the undersea relics of Carthage, the ancient rival to Rome; salvage operations over Roman, Greek, and Phoenician shipwreck sites throughout the Eastern Mediterranean; many dives to the floor of the ocean, examining coral reefs and charting the Gulf of Guinea; and exposing readers to the seemingly limitless wonder of the undersea world of fish (including a very close encounter with a friendly octopus and a hungry shark), mammals, reefs, plants, and shipwrecks. Of the latter, Cousteau says, "The sea allowed each sunken ship to have a personality which is vividly expressed to a diver. In their surface lives, the wrecks have had tragic or comic, dull or adventurous careers."[4]

The most evocative photos in the volume are actually not of the undersea life. Rather, they are the charming shots of Cousteau and his intrepid team of divers. Together they are literally "writing the manual" on how to operate at depth with the new Aqua-Lung technology, risking the many effects on the blood and the brain, which were not well understood. While the undersea photo quality is not remotely what is possible today, these first real images have the same quality as

Matthew Brady photos from the U.S. Civil War years in the infancy of photography. What makes them special is that they were breaking ground in how the world viewed the undersea domain. In a sense, everything had to be invented: the breathing apparatus, the diving suits, the cameras, a sledge to pull gear at depth, the mechanisms to get everything in and out of *Calypso*, and on and on.

Another chapter that reveals a specialized engagement with the sea is on cave diving. In it Cousteau talks about the particularly harrowing and risky deep dives, including what he calls the "worst experience in 5,000 dives at the Fountain of Vaucluse near Avignon." Cousteau describes an accident with the words, "The sky was no longer our business. We belonged now to a world where no light had ever struck."[5] Afflicted with "rapture of the deep," the diving party risked their lives in a series of dives, each of them revealing more of the ancient caves. Another very dangerous dive includes photos of Cousteau and his usual sidekick, Dumas, tangling with several large eight-foot sharks. I'm not a scuba diver but have done my share of snorkeling—enough to know I don't want to be close to serious ocean predators. Cousteau, Dumas, and a huge shark have a pas de trois on the edge of a 12,000-foot ocean abyss off Africa. There are two photographs that chilled my blood, one of the shark heading straight at Cousteau from perhaps ten feet away, the other literally nose-to-nose. Cousteau banged the shark's nose with the camera and it moved away. This led to another invention: the undersea shark cages for observation, which are now so common.

A far more charming encounter, with various octopi, is described in the chapter "Monsters We Have Met." At first Cousteau and his team are wary of the larger octopi but soon discover they are not aggressive or especially interested in them. After many dives they are literally "teaching the octopi" to dance. The photos of "close encounters with an octopus" are worth the price of the book alone. A poignant pair of photos at the end of the book are of a pilot who died in a crash at sea, whose body is discovered by the divers. They raise the body to the surface, with a parachute streaming behind it like a long white shroud.

Following his emergence as an international celebrity after publishing *The Silent World*, Cousteau expanded his work in a wide variety of dimensions. The film adaption of *The Silent World* was wildly well received worldwide and won a Palme d'Or at the Cannes Film Festival in 1956—the first documentary to do so. Also of note was the creation of a weekly television show, *The Undersea World of Jacques Cousteau*, which I loved as a child in the late 1960s. It ran for a decade from 1966 to 1976, and even during my time as a midshipman at Annapolis I would occasionally tune in for an episode. He also created dozens of documentaries and published more than fifty books. In essence, he became a one-man publicity crew for the importance of the oceans, illustrating his views again and again in film, television, and print.

What I particularly admired about Jacques Cousteau was his vitality and energy. If something doesn't exist—invent it! He lived his life very much in the public eye and was unapologetic about his desire for fame. But at the heart of all he did was a simple, obvious, and very real love of the oceans. He loved nothing more than slipping under the waves and descending into the deep sea. We think of aviators, as rendered in the poem "High Flight" by American World War II pilot John Magee, as being those who reach out and touched "the face of God" as they fly up into the air. Jacques-Yves Cousteau, who ironically wanted at one time to be a pilot, found his own "face of God" in the briny deep of the ocean. His enormous legacy has helped the world understand and appreciate the world beneath the waves. *The Silent World* is a fitting testimony to all he shared with us in the long dive of his life.

Bonus: *The Silent World* is the 1956 documentary mentioned above, codirected by Jacques Cousteau and the famous French filmmaker Louis Malle (*Pretty Baby, Atlantic City, My Dinner with Andre,* and many more). It won not only the prestigious Palme d'Or at Cannes, but also an Academy Award. Well worth watching in conjunction with reading the book.

SAILORS IN FICTION

CHAPTER TWENTY-TWO

20,000 LEAGUES UNDER THE SEA

by Jules Verne

The Captain and his men had come to bury their companion in this general resting place, at the bottom of this inaccessible ocean.

—Dr. Pierre Aronnax, *20,000 Leagues under the Sea*[1]

Good science fiction is the merger of advanced and imagined technology alongside a remarkable setting. What makes *20,000 Leagues under the Sea* such a superb novel of the oceans is that it seamlessly combines technology that eventually comes into being, places essentially the entire story underwater, and adds a gripping psychological dimension in the tortured character of Captain Nemo. As I began to assemble this list, I knew it would be part of *The Sailor's Bookshelf* for all three reasons.

The book is set in the mid- to late nineteenth-century, contemporaneous to the times of Jules Verne, a skilled French writer (also author of *Journey to the Centre of the Earth* and *Around the World in 80 Days*). Verne was not a particularly "maritime"-oriented writer, and his first public efforts with a pen were writing librettos for light opera.[2] But beginning in the early 1860s he started to write science fiction and became exceedingly popular, beginning with *Five Weeks in a Balloon*. The novel version of *20,000 Leagues under the Sea* was originally serialized, and the first deluxe single edition appeared in 1871. The book was apparently inspired by Verne viewing an early French submarine, *Plonger*, at an 1867 exposition.

The story opens with a mystery: ships from around the world are reporting sightings of a giant sea monster, possibly a massive whale. A marine scientist, Pierre Aronnax, and his assistant, Conseil, join an expedition to find the monster. Aronnax sails from Manhattan on the U.S. Navy ship *Abraham Lincoln* and meets a Canadian whaler named Ned Land, who becomes his companion throughout the voyage. The three men fall overboard in a confrontation with the monster, which turns out to be the *Nautilus*, the submarine of Captain Nemo. They are taken on board, and so begins the 20,000-league voyage under the world's oceans in which the heroes visit much of the undersea world. They see massive coral formations and sunken warships from antiquarian battles, view the ice formations of Antarctica, sail by the transatlantic telegraph cable, and even see the lost city of Atlantis. They are privileged to sortie outside the skin of the ship on many occasions, including to the funeral described in the quote above. At one point they are attacked by a giant squid and participate in battling it, the most famous scene in the novel.

Looming over the entire narrative is the strange figure of Captain Nemo. We see him never quite in focus. While seemingly sophisticated and reasonably kind to his "guests," he is quite clear with them that they will never be allowed to leave *Nautilus*. The ship appears to be a floating city-state, immune to the legalities and strictures of land-based nations. Nemo's exile from civilization seems self-imposed, and his motivations include scientific research and development as well as the opportunity to attack and sink surface ships when he chooses. There are allusions to a tragedy in his life that resulted in the deaths of his wife and child at the hands of an unnamed militaristic state (which some critics believe was the Russian Empire, with Nemo appearing as a Polish nobleman in early drafts of the book). Late in the novel, *Nautilus* is attacked by a warship, possibly from the nation that caused Nemo so much suffering, and he destroys the vessel by ramming it.

After this incident, Nemo seems more detached from his mission. There is a lack of purpose felt throughout the crew, and the ship meanders around the world under the seven seas. Eventually the three protagonists manage to escape, although the fate of *Nautilus* is unclear as the final scene at sea has the massive submarine caught in a maelstrom and headed for the bottom of the ocean. The book is most powerful in its vision of the fleets of undersea nuclear-powered submarines, which it clearly and accurately predicted nearly a full century before they were fully operational. It is also a moving tribute to the pure beauty of the undersea world, and some writers have called it a sort of early ecowarrior adventure in which Nemo heroically rejects nations and their ocean-damaging industrial activities.

The book also provides insight into the pressures and isolation of command at sea, much like Joseph Conrad's short story "The Secret Sharer." Nemo can indulge his whims for both research and revenge equally and lives in an essentially unbounded universe. When I asked U.S. Navy captain Ned Beach (captain of the fifth Navy nuclear submarine *Triton* and author of the World War II submarine classic *Run Silent, Run Deep*) about the best books for the submarine force, the first one he mentioned was *20,000 Leagues under the Sea*. When I asked him why he would include a novel of French science fiction over a century old, he said simply, "Because Captain Nemo was the first real captain of a submarine and showed us both how rewarding and how difficult it could be."

The story has been turned into film, stage and even graphic novels. Interestingly, Nemo's nationality shifts in the book's sequel (which is far less readable), *The Mysterious Island*. In the latter, he has become East Indian, as he appears in several of the films. In the graphic novel series *The League of Extraordinary*

Gentlemen by Alan Moore and Kevin O'Neill, Nemo is also of Asian appearance. Taken in whatever form you choose, *20,000 Leagues under the Sea* is a classic work of sea literature and one of the very few in the genre of science fiction that has so perfectly withstood the test of time.

Bonus: The 1954 movie stars Kirk Douglas as the harpooner Ned Land and James Mason as Captain Nemo. It incorporates plot lines from both *20,000 Leagues under the Sea* and the sequel, *The Mysterious Island*. The special effects are quite advanced for the time, and it won two Academy Awards. It was personally produced by Walt Disney. The graphic novel series *The League of Extraordinary Gentlemen* also features a great deal of Captain Nemo and is well done.

CHAPTER
TWENTY-THREE

MASTER AND
COMMANDER

by Patrick O'Brian

Walking down at a quarter to one, walking down to the
waterside . . . he felt a curious shortness of his breath . . .
"am I afraid?" he wondered.[1]

I began reading the sea novels of Patrick O'Brian in the mid-1990s, when a captain of a warship for the first time myself. I had a collection of fairly tattered paperback copies of the first dozen or so of the twenty full-length novels in the entire series. I would sit in my chair on the starboard side of the bridge when things were quiet at sea and read them. My watch officers would see me intently focused on the books, stifling a laugh here and there, utterly absorbed in each of the books. Soon my officers were asking to borrow the paperbacks after I finished them, and in time the entire wardroom of twenty-five officers was engrossed in the seagoing (and land faring) adventures of Royal Navy captain Jack Aubrey and ship's surgeon, Stephen Maturin. On our longer voyages in my destroyer *Barry*, we would often discuss the latest turn of events or point out that we were sailing at that moment through a particular body of water mentioned in one of the books: the Strait of Gibraltar, the Eastern Mediterranean, or pulling into Portsmouth, England.

Eventually, after well over two years in command and having sailed tens of thousands of sea miles, it came time for me to go ashore and on to the next step in my long voyage as a naval officer. As is traditional, the executive officer (second in command) then-lieutenant commander Mike Franken hosted a drinks party ashore for Laura and me. It was a very warm affair with kind toasts both ways between me and the wardroom. Normally the departing captain receives a small gift, perhaps with a nautical theme—a barometer or a nautical chronometer or some such. A large box was trundled out by one of the ensigns, and I opened it to find a complete set of Patrick O'Brian's novels. Mike Franken (who went on to be a vice admiral in a very successful career, by the way), pulled out the final volume in the set at that time, which was titled simply *The Commodore*. That was the next logical step for me, to command not a single destroyer but a group of six or seven of them in a squadron. Mike said, "It's a good omen for you, captain," and opened the book to show me it was a first edition signed by Patrick O'Brian himself. That book remains a cornerstone in my library, and every time I pick it up I smile and think of *Barry*, and sea duty, and the long horizon of the ocean as I sat in that chair on the bridge wing devouring those books.

Patrick O'Brian at first seems an unlikely author of what many believe is the finest set of novels about the sea in history. He shrouded his life in mystery for years; his real name was Richard Patrick Russ, and he was born in England in 1914. While he unsuccessfully applied to attend the Royal Naval College, in Dartmouth, England, in the 1920s, he never served in the navy. In 1945 he legally changed his name to a very Irish-sounding Patrick O'Brian. While he claimed to have some sailing experience, he never successfully demonstrated it to anyone. Instead, he was a writer with an interest in nature, decidedly more like Maturin (the landlubber, Irish-Catalonia physician and spy chief utterly lost at sea) instead of Aubrey (a thorough sea dog of a Royal Navy officer with zero aptitude for life ashore). His series on the two eventually achieved cult status, and in his seventies O'Brian improbably became a highly paid speaker with each of his novels highly anticipated among legions of fans (including this one). He died in Ireland just after the turn of the century, January 2000, and is buried in southern France. Over the course of his long life, he became a self-taught expert on the Napoleonic-era Royal Navy; the rigging of sailing warships; the splicing of knots; the surgical procedures of the time; the Latin names for the many species of birds, fish, and animals that Maturin encounters; and a thousand other relatively obscure aspects of seagoing life.

I chose the first book in O'Brian's twenty-volume series even though several others perhaps surpass it in narrative drive; but in this reading endeavor, it is best to begin at the beginning. *Master and Commander* opens in the spring of 1800 in the British port of Mahon on the island of Minorca. Captain Jack and Surgeon Stephen are attending a musical entertainment at the governor's house, where they almost come to furious blows and contemplate a duel. Fortunately for readers, Jack learns later that night that he will take command for the first time of the "sweet sailing" sloop *Sophie*, a small warship of fourteen guns—but a huge step for Jack. Taking command is his heart's desire and most importantly affords the opportunity to take prizes and become rich. After ship command, his greatest passion is money. He invites Maturin to become his ship's surgeon (normally such a small ship would not have a physician), and the penniless Maturin agrees. Thus launches two thousand pages across the twenty novels in the series.

The plot of *Master and Commander* revolves around a series of set pieces at sea, culminating in the battle *Sophie* fights against a much larger Spanish warship, a very maneuverable ship of thirty-two guns known as a "xebec-frigate." After this victory Jack still manages to run afoul with his chain of command by initiating an affair with the wife of his immediate superior. We see the theme of Jack's supreme competency at sea and complete foolery ashore that is a running leitmotif throughout the entire series. Stephen, on the other hand, is incredibly competent ashore—speaks many languages, is an accomplished surgeon and naturalist, a deadly pistol shot and skilled swordsman in a duel—but a complete "booby" at sea. *Sophie* has several other seagoing encounters, but by the end of the novel is captured by an overwhelming force of French ships. Jack faces a court-martial, as is required under British naval regulations for being captured, but at the very end of the novel is acquitted.

Picking up *Master and Commander* is truly to embark on a meditation on friendship and shipmates; command of an enterprise; the foibles that plague us all, albeit in differing ways; and—above all—the omnipresent nature of the sea. People often say the novels are about a lifelong friendship between Aubrey and Maturin, but in my mind's eye, it is a ménage à trois, a triangle relationship between Jack, Stephen, and the sea itself. What sustains the books through such a long, long voyage is the way the ocean presents fresh challenges, seemingly on every page. The resilience of the crews of Jack's various ships throughout the series is remarkable, as are his own responses to the failures he suffers at sea and ashore. In the end, long after Patrick O'Brian has sailed on across that distant sea we all must cross one day, his characters—Jack, Stephen, and the sea itself—continue the voyage. You can join one anytime by picking up this extraordinary book.

Bonus: The 2003 film *Master and Commander: The Far Side of the World,* starring Russell Crowe as Capt. Jack Aubrey and Paul Bettany as Dr. Stephen Maturin, is excellent. The title is a mash-up of two of the books, and the plot is not exclusive to either. Rather, the film, cowritten and directed by Peter Weir, sought to provide a highly visual exposition of the books. Notably, there is very little dialog in the movie—instead, the story is told through haunting music and incredibly realistic photography. Reflecting this, of the ten Academy Award nominations the film received, it won in two categories: cinematography and sound. It lost the Best Picture award that year to the final installment of the *Lord of the Rings* saga, which was indeed high competition. Watching the film before diving into the book is a terrific scene-setter and well worth the lengthy running time of well over two hours (138 minutes).

CHAPTER TWENTY-FOUR

MISTER ROBERTS

by Thomas Heggen

The Captain of a naval vessel is a curious affair. Personally, he may be short, scrawny, unprepossessing; but a Captain is not a person and cannot be viewed as such. He is an embodiment. He is given stature, substance, and sometimes a new dimension by the massive, cumulative authority of the Navy Department which looms behind him like a shadow. With some Captains this shadow is a great, terrifying cloud; with others, it is scarcely apparent at all: but with none can it go unnoticed.[1]

When I was a brand-new ensign, U.S. Navy, fresh out of Annapolis, I was lucky enough to be sent to an equally brand-new ship: the *Spruance*-class destroyer, USS *Hewitt*. She was the fourth of the class, and because the ship was new, it had a hand-picked crew and wardroom who had participated in the commissioning of the ship and were therefore called, in Navy tradition, "plank owners," connoting ownership of a metaphorical plank in the new ship. As the first non–plank owner to report to the ship and as a green ensign, I received more than a little ribbing from the much more experienced officers in the wardroom. Hewitt also had a very tough-minded, old-fashioned sea dog of a captain who could be very hard on new ensigns, including Ensign Stavridis.

Fortunately for me, I worked for Lt. Jerry Farrell, the ship's very experienced operations officer. Farrell would go on to a highly successful naval career, commanding several ships, including a cruiser, and to service as the deputy commandant at Annapolis, from which he had graduated himself. Lieutenant Farrell reminded me a lot of Lt. Doug Roberts, the hero of *Mister Roberts*: he was deeply skilled at his craft, from shiphandling to scheduling; endlessly willing to mentor younger officers and crewmembers; and willing to provide some protective cover from the CO when necessary. He also had a fine sense of humor. Like Ensign Pulver in *Mister Roberts*, I had a lot to learn and did not always make the best choices. Eventually I would get my sea legs, of course, but for the rest of my career (and especially as a mid-grade officer) I tried to help and mentor others just as Farrell had done for me. Mentorship is the heart of this fine novel, which is extremely comic at times and also has a very serious heart to it.

While I didn't have the "full Mister Roberts" experience, it was close enough to endear both the book and the equally good movie to me. The novel came out in 1946, and the film appeared much later, in 1955. In between was a successful Broadway play, and later there was also a short-lived television series in the mid-1960s. The plotline of all four track closely together, and the story of *Mister Roberts* is based fairly closely on the wartime experiences of author Thomas Heggen on board USS *Virgo*, a logistic ship similar to the ship that is the centerpiece of the novel. The central theme of the book is actually simple: ideals and character are vitally important in a world that is constantly shifting under our feet (like a ship at sea). The story is also about the most important role of any leader, which in the end is to make new leaders—and how especially important that is in the tiny, confined universe of a ship at sea.

The book opens with the wardroom and crew of an auxiliary cargo ship, the USS *Reluctant*, plying their boring logistic work sailing from "Apathy to Tedium, with occasional side trips to Monotony and Ennui."[2] While the work is critical to keep the forward fighting fleet supplied, Lt. Doug Roberts constantly chafes under the very poor leadership of an incompetent and truculent captain, wishing he could get into the action. Roberts pines to serve in a destroyer or cruiser, but—as the *Reluctant*'s first lieutenant—he is central to the successful completion of the mission. While Roberts hates the ship and the captain, he knows he has a duty to perform in keeping the supplies flowing and the wardroom and crew as buffered as possible from the commanding officer.

The novel is essentially a series of vignettes depicting life on the ship—raucous liberty runs ashore by the crew, childish pranks and feuds between the officers, and a series of minor mini-mutinies (including throwing palm trees overboard) against the commanding officer, Lieutenant Commander Morton. Roberts keeps requesting transfer to a combatant and eventually gains his wish with the surreptitious cooperation of the crew—but sadly is killed shortly thereafter. Ensign Pulver then comes into his own, fulfilling the thematic point of the book—that leaders must create new leaders who can follow behind them.

Unlike many of the "classic" World War II epic novels by James Jones, Norman Mailer, Herman Wouk, and many others, *Mister Roberts* is a small book with a very tight setting. It also differs from most World War II literature in that it employs a great deal of humor while making some of the same deadly serious points that appear in other World War II classics like *From Here to Eternity* or *The Winds of War*. *Mister Roberts* is full of irony. At the end, Ensign Pulver, while drinking coffee in the wardroom, learns of the death of Lieutenant Roberts, who is killed in a kamikaze attack on the destroyer to which he finally was transferred. The moment crystalizes something in Pulver, and the ensign goes to the captain's cabin to find him reading: "The Captain was sitting, reading, in the large chair of his cabin. In the cone of harsh light from the floor lamp he looked old, and not evil, but merely foolish. 'Yeah,' he said gruffly, 'what is it?' Ensign Pulver leaned a casual hand on the door jamb. 'Captain,' he said easily, 'I just threw your damn palm trees over the side.'" At that moment, Mister Roberts's work is done, as is his story. But the spirit of leadership at sea lives on and deserves its place on *The Sailor's Bookshelf*.

Bonus: The 1955 movie *Mister Roberts* was quite successful and included Henry Fonda in a master turn as Roberts, a young Jack Lemmon as Pulver, and a scratchy-sounding James Cagney as Captain Morton. Directed by John Ford, it was nominated for three Academy Awards, and Jack Lemmon won Best Supporting Actor for his role.

CHAPTER TWENTY-FIVE

MOBY-DICK OR, THE WHALE

by Herman Melville

There is, one knows not what sweet mystery about this sea,
whose gently awful stirrings seem to speak of some
hidden soul beneath. . . .
Both jaws, like enormous shears, bit the craft
completely in twain. . . .
It is not down on any map; true places never are. . . .
I know not all that may be coming, but be it what it will,
I'll go to it laughing.[1]

In my home are five copies of *Moby-Dick, or the Whale*, which was published in 1851 to so-so reviews. Yet I consider it the greatest novel of the sea ever written, and I have returned to read it again and again over the years, certainly not each time plumbing the depth of its hundreds of pages. Time and again I return to favorite sections and quotes like the four above, which I've chosen for the way they illuminate the crucial points Melville made.

Many critics have described this not only as the greatest of maritime novels but as the singularly "great American novel"—a description that itself is a bit of an obsessive search by reviewers and for which there are many other worthy contenders, to be sure.

Melville had been to sea himself around the middle of the nineteenth century. He'd served several years in the unique part of the business represented by whaling ships, which in those days sought the sperm whale principally to harvest its oil. This was brutally hard work, and very dangerous. The central story line of *Moby-Dick* is loosely based on the destruction of a whaling ship, *Essex*, in 1820 (and is the subject of Nathaniel Philbrick's brilliant work of nonfiction, *In the Heart of the Sea*, also a book on *The Sailor's Bookshelf*).

The plot is big and rendered in prose that at times is quite pedestrian, verging on pedantic (in long segments about whales and whaling) but in other parts soars to beautiful rhetorical heights that echo Shakespeare and the King James Bible. There are asides that read almost as stage direction, as well as sea shanties and bits of poetry. It is not an easy book to read in many places, and when I taught it as part of a literature of the sea class at Tufts University in the early 1980s, I spent a lot of time simply encouraging my undergraduate students to stay with it. Once a reader has climbed the mountain of *Moby-Dick*, it is a book that stays with you forever, especially in terms of understanding the oceans. Like the sea itself, this epic novel will get into the heart of a reader who is open to its unique structure and tone.

So, what happens? The narrator, Ishmael (the opening line, "Call me Ishmael," is one of the most famous openings in literature), arrives in New Bedford, Massachusetts, looking for a ship. He meets another immortal character, a Polynesian whaler named Queequeg, at an inn. There is a whaling museum in New Bedford today, where I shepherded my students to let them begin at the beginning, so to speak.[2] Despite several ominous signals, Ishmael and Queequeg sign on to a ship named *Pequod* to serve under Captain Ahab, an "ungodly, god-like man." On board they meet not only the irascible captain but his officers. Chief among them is the name from the novel that has become the most famous of all, as it adorns over 30,000 coffeeshops around the world: Starbuck. And yes, the company's name is an echo of that doomed first mate—just look at your

Starbucks' cup to see the nautical theme mermaid or siren. The company was almost named Pequod, by the way. I'm glad they chose Starbucks.

After the ship gets under way, Ahab limps out to the quarterdeck. He lost his leg to the "white whale" from the knee down and is sporting a crutch made out of the jawbone of another whale. In a famous scene, he nails a gold piece to the mast and says he will give it to any sailor who sights the white whale. *Pequod* continues south from Nantucket where Ishmael boarded and heads east, headed to the Pacific by rounding southern Africa. Near the Cape of Good Hope *Pequod* interrogates another ship, one of a series of such encounters. All of them portend the coming disaster, from crewmembers going insane to the deaths of other, smaller whales to Ahab's dropped speaking trumpet. One of the encounters is with another sea captain named Boomer who, like Ahab, has lost a limb to Moby Dick (his arm). But, unlike Ahab, he has not descended into an obsessive hatred of the beast. All of this is included in an almost-constant set of observations about the oceans, whales, their habits, navigation, typhoons and other weather phenomena, crew morale at sea, the spirit of fire, and dozens of other stories and ideas from Ishmael. The whaler *Rachel* makes an appearance, again with a portent of doom, in this case a search for the captain's son, who was lost overboard—a search that Ahab refuses to join in his unseemly haste to get to Moby Dick.

Even an encounter with an ironically named whaler *Delight*, which had just been badly damaged by Moby Dick, fails to deter Ahab, and as the novel nears its climax, a sea hawk snatches the captain's hat off his head and flies to sea with it. The final encounter with *Delight* concludes with her captain prophetically saying that there is no harpoon ever forged that can kill Moby Dick.

At this point *Pequod* encounters the white whale, and a three-day chase ensures—despite Starbuck's entreaty to the captain to return home to Nantucket. Ahab "smells" the whale, sees it first, and claims the gold piece he nailed to the mast. While chasing the whale on the first day, his personal longboat is crushed by the whale, although Ahab survives. The second day brings more disaster as three additional longboats are destroyed by the whale, and Ahab loses his artificial limb into the sea. The third and final day begins with a noon sighting of the whale, and Moby Dick destroys another two boats. Ahab manages to spear the back of the whale, but Moby Dick destroys the final longboat and then attacks the *Pequod* itself. The whale and Ahab conduct a final confrontation, which ends with Ahab dragged into the sea by the line connected to the harpoon, which has become entangled around his neck. The two of them disappear as the whale sounds. As *Pequod* sinks in a vortex, a coffin shoots to the surface, and Ishmael manages to swim to it and survives floating at sea. A day later the whaler *Rachel* rescues him, the last survivor of the doomed *Pequod*.

As both a writer and a former sea captain, it is difficult to overstate the magnitude of Melville's accomplishment. The themes that are woven through this classic include the relationship of mankind with the oceans and the ultimate victory of nature; the racial mix of the United States in the mid-nineteenth century; the nature of obsession and how it can doom our lives; and a dozen other important ideas. If we can agree that, in so many ways, the United States is an island nation—buffered from the world by vast oceans—then the case for *Moby-Dick* as the ultimate American novel is very strong. Others will say that our history and national character have not been as strongly shaped by the sea as by the development of the West and the conquest of the land—making a case for novels like Cormac McCarthy's *Blood Meridian*. But again and again, as I read and reread *Moby-Dick*, I see that so much of what we think of as the American character is in fact related to the ocean—its vast space, its heartless natural forces, the sense of limitless motion, the need to conquer it with independence and strength, our dangerous tendency to obsess over challenges, the science and technology that undergird our nation's progress, even in this turbulent twenty-first century.

There is so much more to be said about this challenging, magnificent, maddening work of literature, but in closing this brief synopsis I would offer two thoughts. First, this is a fundamental work of not only sea literature but of the literature of the human spirit in all its complex incarnations. Like the canon of Shakespeare, it must be read in the context of the human voyage through life. And second, the connections of mankind to the uncaring but ever-present sea are truly more vivid here than in any other book of fiction I have ever read. This is, of course, a sailor's book but also one that offers the deepest of lessons and ideas even to those who have never even glimpsed the waves.

Bonus: *Moby-Dick* can be read in sections and chapters, and don't be discouraged if parts of it are too dense with detail or simply boring to the reader—skip ahead. And a way to fully appreciate it is to first read Nathaniel Philbrick's extraordinary history of the 1820 incident that probably inspired Melville to write the book. Philbrick, a gifted historian with a particular feel for the sea (he lives on Nantucket and is an accomplished off shore sailor), makes *In the Heart of the Sea* truly come alive, and he beautifully prepares the reader for *Moby-Dick*.

CHAPTER TWENTY-SIX

MOODS OF THE SEA
Masterworks of Sea Poetry

by George C. Solley and Eric Steinbaugh

And as the smart ship grew
In stature, grace, and hue
In shadowy silent distance grew the Iceberg too[1]

A nyone who looks out across a lonely beach at a gray, churning sea is looking at a poem. Indeed, that distant point where the sea meets the sky is,
in many ways, a perfect poetic metaphor for eternity, and it calls to
us. The poetry of the sea helps explain why many of us are so drawn toward seascapes when entering a museum of art; why we can sit quietly hour after hour in
a deck chair and examine the distant horizon; or how the ever-changing face of
the ocean attracts us so deeply. There are seemingly endless poems written about
the world's oceans, and they deserve a place on any sailor's bookshelf.

For me, poetry and the sea have always been intertwined. The oceans have
their own discrete rhythms—tides, currents, winds, rising and setting suns,

moons, and stars—that provide symmetry even as they inspire the eye and the ear. Good poetry has much the same quality wherein the whole is so much greater than the sum of the parts. The sea and poetry have always been twin passions of mine. The challenge has been finding the poems and coherently collecting and structuring them. For years, I tried to do that, copying or clipping good sea poems where I found them and collecting a fairly thick manila folder into which I would dip from time to time. Fortunately, as I began teaching a "Literature of the Sea" class at Tufts University in the early 1980s, a single volume emerged that did a super job collecting, organizing, and illuminating sea poetry. Compiled by a pair of Marine Corps junior officers on the English literature faculty at Annapolis, *Moods of the Sea* is a near-perfect compendium of sea poetry.

While focused almost entirely on British and American poets, the collection still has a global feel given the breadth and depth of the selections, including portions of Homer's *Odyssey*, the earliest tale of a long sea voyage home; the Bible (so many beautiful psalms that celebrate the sea); Shakespeare (*The Tempest*, of course, but also *Henry V* and *Richard III*); Samuel Taylor Coleridge ("The Rime of the Ancient Mariner," in its lengthy entirety); Alfred, Lord Tennyson ("Ulysses," one of the most moving of sea poems); and dozens of others. John Keats, Rudyard Kipling, Herman Melville, D. H. Lawrence, Langston Hughes, Lord Byron, James Fenimore Cooper, Robert Louis Stevenson, Walt Whitman, Robert Frost, and Edna St. Vincent Millay all make multiple appearances.

The poems are cleverly grouped in six sections: Sounds of the Sea; Man and the Sea; Tales of the Sea; The Laughter of the Waves; Legends of the Sea; and a final catch-all that contains many of the most evocative works, "The Sea as Metaphor." The authors avoided overly specific thematic divisions—for example, "shipwrecks" or "dawn at sea"—in favor of the half dozen general categories above. It works beautifully and brings together clusters of poems that reinforce each other in many ways. Once you pick up the volume, it becomes hard to put down.

Two sea poems that have also stood out for me as a former sea captain are "The Convergence of the Twain: Lines on the Loss of the Titanic" by Thomas Hardy; and "Ulysses," by Alfred, Lord Tennyson. The first is a very short, elegant, and haunting poem about the collision of the Titanic and the iceberg that would eventually sink it. In very brief snapshots, Hardy evokes the construction of the beautiful ship in the British shipyard, gradually coming to life as a supposedly unsinkable vessel, ready to transport the glamorous passengers across the Atlantic. He alternates that construction and "coming to life" with a vision of the iceberg growing in size and scale and drifting across the dark, cold ocean. Eventually, of course, the two converge, with tragic results. For any captain who has stood a long night watch on his or her ship, it is a poem worth reciting from time to time.

Even more powerful is Tennyson's story of the voyage of Ulysses back to his home island after long years at sea, only to discover that he will always continue to yearn for the sea and the vast unknown world that a journey on the oceans provides. The final stanzas hit deeply home to anyone who has spent significant time on the deep ocean but has finally left it for the comforts of home and hearth—the heart continues to want the vast expanse of the sea. In the poem, Ulysses lays out the case for going again to sea, whatever the stage of life in which we find ourselves:

There lies the port; the vessel puffs her sail;
There gloom the dark broad seas.
The lights begin to twinkle from the rocks;
The long day wanes; the slow moon climbs; the deep
Moans round with many voices. Come my friends,
Tis not too late to seek a newer world.
Push off, and sitting well in order smite
The sounding furrows; for my purpose holds
To sail beyond the sunset, and the baths
Of all the western stars, until I die.[2]

The lines above give a beautiful image of yearning for the sea that sticks in the mind of anyone who has sailed the oceans. It is but one example of a poem that captures how many sailors feel about their time at sea, and the lifelong desire many feel to go down again and again to the sea in ships. What a sea voyage offers in the end is a powerful and unique *experience*. Ulysses speaks for us all when he says,

I am a part of all that I have met;
Yet all experience is an arch wherethrough
Gleams that untraveled world whose margin fades
Forever and forever when I move.[3]

Even though we may find ourselves shore bound as our lives unfold, through the poetry of the sea, we can always sail through that arc of experience and find our way to the untraveled world. This beautifully realized survey of sea poetry provides a well-charted course to sail.

CHAPTER TWENTY-SEVEN

MUTINY ON THE BOUNTY

by Charles Nordhoff and James Norman Hall

Sign it instantly! Damme! I am not the most
patient man in the world.

— Capt. William Bligh of HMS *Bounty*[1]

O ver the years, I had a few encounters with the story of *Mutiny on the Bounty*, including reading the novel and at one point seeing the movie, with Marlon Brando in the role of First Mate Fletcher Christian and Trevor Howard as Captain Bligh (I don't recommend the movie, by the way). But when the extraordinary nature of the story really came home to me vividly was in 1994 when I was a ship's captain myself in a Navy destroyer, USS *Barry*. We were assigned to be part of the marking of the fiftieth anniversary of D-Day, which meant sailing across the Atlantic and docking in Portsmouth, England, home of the Royal Navy. We made it pier-side easily enough after a very rough night at sea in the English Channel. I was ready to dive into the long and distinguished history of the British navy, which is fully on display in Portsmouth. After spending an afternoon touring the incredibly impressive HMS *Victory*, Vice Admiral Nelson's flagship, I went over to the main building of the Portsmouth Naval Shipyard Museum, alongside of which *Victory* reposes. The entire complex is an amazing maritime museum. It is one of the finest of its kind in the world, and I've seen dozens over the years.

As I was wandering through the displays, I came across a small sailing boat, essentially a launch or a longboat. The placards indicated it was a model of the boat in which the mutinous crew of the *Bounty* set their captain adrift in 1789. After the mutiny, Capt. William Bligh and nineteen loyalists navigated without a chart or any means of determining longitude, yet managed to sail forty-seven days and cover 3,600 miles in that small, open craft. They finally made it to Coupang on the island of Timor on June 17, 1789. By March 14 of the following year, he had made it to Portsmouth and published his account. As I stared at that boat, a bit over twenty feet long, it seemed impossible to me that anyone could have sailed it a distance greater than crossing the entire United States of America. It is a stunning feat of navigation, but an even more surprising one of leadership under extreme stress.

After seeing the launch, I returned to reread the novel *Mutiny on the Bounty* as well as the following two volumes, *Men against the Sea* and *Pitcairn's Island*. All three books are powerful stories of leadership successes and failures, the fickle character of human nature when it is tempted by a softer and better life, endurance and resilience in the most extreme circumstances, and life at sea. The novels roughly follow the true-life events of the mutiny itself (*Mutiny on the Bounty*), Bligh's epic sea voyage (*Men against the Sea*), and the final chapters of the saga (*Pitcairn's Island*). Together they are collectively known as the "Bounty Trilogy" and often are published in a sort of omnibus, although I own original single volumes of each.

Mutiny on the Bounty is told through the eyes of Roger Byam, a midshipman and serving linguist who lays out the tyranny and abusive leadership of William Bligh. The *Bounty* sailed for the South Pacific in 1787 to gather breadfruit trees and to conduct general navigation and language research. The conditions on the ship are terrible, and Bligh embitters the crew with his harsh treatment and corporal punishment, petty corruption, and refusal to address any of their concerns.

Still, *Bounty* makes it to Tahiti and begins to fulfill its missions. The real trouble starts as the crewmembers discover how idyllic life can be with the promiscuous local women. Yet the captain manages to get them back on board the ship and under way for the next stop, the Caribbean. As they are sailing back, Bligh's behavior reaches new levels of incoherence and anger, and he accuses some in the crew of stealing coconuts. Fletcher Christian turns against him and leads the mutiny. Bligh and eighteen loyalists are set adrift in a small launch with the almost certainty they will die at sea. His last words to the crew, delivered from the small boat before it is cast off, are indicative of the man: "'I know you to be a bloody scoundrel!' he shouted, shaking his fist in Christian's direction. 'But I'll have vengeance! Mind that, you ungrateful villain! I'll see you swinging at a yard-arm before two years have passed! And every traitor with you!'"

Bounty returns to Tahiti, where Christian lets those who wish to leave the ship, including Byam, go ashore. Christian then sails the *Bounty* in search of a deserted and uncharted island to avoid the long arm of British naval justice that he knows is looming. Eventually the Royal Navy sends a vessel to capture the mutineers, and Byam is captured and imprisoned before being taken back to Great Britain. After various legal maneuvers and a near completion of a death sentence, Byam is saved in the nick of time when a friend corroborates his claims of innocence during the actual mutiny. Improbably, Byam eventually rises in the Royal Navy and becomes a captain himself. On a voyage, he learns that the Tahitian woman he loved and "married" is dead, but he meets the daughter he had with her.

The sequel, *Men against the Sea*, is the story of the open-boat voyage of former captain Willian Bligh and his fellow eighteen loyalists. It was published in 1934 as a hard-cover novel and is told from the point of view of Thomas Ledward, the acting surgeon of *Bounty*. In the boat with Bligh and Ledward are officers and senior petty officers, including the sailing master, master's mate, carpenter, botanist, and boatswain. All are experienced seamen and are willing to work together to survive. The final book in the trilogy, *Pitcairn's Island*, was also published in book form in 1934 and completes the story of the mutineers. *Bounty*, under the command of Fletcher Christian, tries to settle on the island of Tubuai but then returns to Tahiti. Christian and eight Englishmen plus eighteen Polynesians left Tahiti in 1789 and essentially vanished. In 1808, nearly two decades later, an American merchant sailing vessel found a robust community on Pitcairn Island under the leadership of a British man who went by the name of "Alexander Smith." Today there are still about forty descendants of the mutineers and the Polynesians, and the burned out hull of *Bounty* can still be seen.

All three of the novels are well worth the read, but the best in the context of sea literature is the first, *Mutiny on the Bounty*. The cross-cutting personalities in the novel, largely modeled on history, connect with the challenges of the sea. But both *Men against the Sea* and *Pitcairn's Island* also offer valuable insights on the seagoing life.

Bonus: The 1962 film version of *Mutiny on the Bounty* was a box office bomb, and deservedly so. The 1984 version (*The Bounty*) is much better, ably directed by Ronald Donaldson, with Mel Gibson as Fletcher Christian and Anthony Hopkins as Captain Bligh. It has very high production values (including an amazingly accurate model of *Bounty*) and a cast that boasts five past and future Academy Award winners among them: Gibson, Hopkins, Liam Neeson, Sir Laurence Olivier, and Daniel Day-Lewis. It is terrific.

CHAPTER TWENTY-EIGHT

RUN SILENT, RUN DEEP

by Edward L. Beach

Sea Power now refers to irresistible onslaught from the
deep of the sea, capable of such terrible visitation as to
amount to a whole war in a single day.[1]

I first met Capt. Edward "Ned" Beach at the U.S. Naval Institute in Annapolis when I was a lieutenant commander. I was receiving a prize for an article I'd published in *Proceedings* magazine, the official publication of the Institute and essentially the "journal of record" of the sea services. Captain Beach was attending the same annual meeting, a gathering held on a rotating basis between Annapolis, Monterey, and Newport in those days. I was in my early thirties and had just finished up a third sea tour, and I was feeling pretty salty. Then I saw Captain Beach. I knew his biography a bit and had read a couple of his books by then, including *Run Silent, Run Deep*, a cult classic in the submarine force and a national best seller.[2] Captain Beach was beyond salty; he was briny, he was crusty, and he looked to me like a middle-weight fighter who had been a trident-bearer for King Neptune.

We chatted for a few minutes, and he struck me a bit like Humphrey Bogart—a real 1950s man: short, quick responses; a tendency to correct anything he felt wasn't quite up to snuff; and clearly not suffering fools (or junior lieutenant commanders) lightly. His lovely and gracious wife, Ingrid, helped keep the conversation moving, and over the next half hour and a good glass of scotch, I came to deeply appreciate this legendary sailor. Among the most decorated diesel submariners in World War II, he made a dozen combat patrols and received many decorations, the highest among them the Navy Cross (just below the Medal of Honor in precedence). An Annapolis graduate, he ranked at the very top of his class (2nd of 576) and was a surface warfare officer before heading to submarine school (where he predictably graduated first in his class). His World War II service included time in the submarines *Trigger*, *Tirante*, and *Piper*. As executive officer (second in command) of *Tirante* he received the Navy Cross, and his commanding officer was awarded the Medal of Honor.

After the war Beach had a series of high-visibility assignments, including command of the *Amberjack*, an advanced technology diesel boat; naval aide to the first chairman of the Joint Chiefs of Staff; command of a second new diesel boat, *Trigger*; and four years as the naval aide to President Dwight Eisenhower. After being promoted early to captain, he returned to sea to command an oiler, *Salamonie*, before heading to nuclear power school to qualify for command of a nuclear submarine, *Triton*. Beach took *Triton* on her "shake-down" (initial) cruise in 1959 and circumnavigated the earth underwater over 41,000 miles the following year. Despite a sterling record of sea service, he was never selected to flag rank, something I have never understood. Perhaps his career was simply TOO glamorous when you add in the reason he resides on *The Sailor's Bookshelf*: in addition to being a perfect seagoing naval officer, he was also a gifted writer.

Perhaps the writing ran in the blood; his father was a writer too (as well as a famous naval officer of his time). Ned Beach's first book was *Submarine!*, which came out in 1952 to excellent reviews. But it was his first novel, *Run Silent, Run Deep*, that cemented his fame as a writer. Appearing in 1955, it was on the *New York Times* best-seller list for months and was (loosely) the basis for a movie starring Clark Gable and Burt Lancaster in 1958. Beach eventually wrote two more novels and a total of thirteen books in his long and productive life as a writer.

Of all his books (and several others *could* have made this list), I chose *Run Silent, Run Deep* because it so perfectly captures the World War II ethos of the "silent service" diesel boat force that still drives today's nuclear submarine Navy. It is written as a transcript of a taped interview by Cdr. Ed Richardson discussing his Medal of Honor performance in combat. The book follows Richardson through his command tour, with Lt. Jim Bledsoe as his executive officer. After their boat is outfitted, Richardson and Bledsoe head to sea—but Richardson is forced to withdraw his "command recommendation" for Bledsoe after a performance failure. In their patrols they encounter a deadly Japanese destroyer, captained by "Bungo Pete" who has sunk a string of diesel boats. This leads to Richardson becoming wounded and reversing himself on Bledsoe, recommending him for command of their boat while Richardson recovers in hospital.

Bledsoe does well in command but has an extramarital affair in Pearl Harbor, causing Richardson to yet again revise his views of the young, aggressive executive officer. The boat is sunk by Bungo Pete, and Richardson recovers to take a new command to sea, the *Eel*. In that submarine, he goes up against Bungo Pete and sinks the Japanese flotilla, personally killing his opponent by ramming his lifeboat. The story ends with Richardson receiving the Medal of Honor and going home with the hope of seeing Laura, the wife of Bledsoe, who had been an object of desire (although unfulfilled, for ethical reasons) for him throughout the novel.

What makes this such a superb depiction of seagoing operations is the specialized aspects of submarine warfare. To fully understand the oceans, we need to appreciate what goes on not only on the surface and in the air above but what lurks in the depths. And it is not just the marine creatures so beautifully illuminated by Jacques Cousteau in *The Silent World*. Today there are metal monsters below, which can launch nuclear-tipped ballistic missiles, sink virtually any surface ship with fast-running torpedoes, and conduct the most delicate of intelligence and surveillance missions. *Run Silent, Run Deep* lays out that part of *The Sailor's Bookshelf* better than any other single volume. On the subject of submarines, the extremely gifted naval officer and writer Ned Beach literally wrote the book, and it deserves a close read.

Bonus: The film version of *Run Silent, Run Deep* is not particularly good, and Ned Beach told me he hated it. A far better submarine movie is *Das Boot* (The Boat), a German movie about a diesel boat in World War II; the novel is excellent as well. Another fine film is *The Hunt for Red October*, which climaxes in a cat-and-mouse chase between U.S. and Soviet submarines. Based on the best-selling novel by Tom Clancy, it is a far better depiction of the subsurface world.

CHAPTER
TWENTY-NINE

SHORT STORIES OF THE SEA

by George C. Solley and Eric Steinbaugh,
with introduction and biographies by David O. Tomlinson

I thought the time had come to declare myself.
I am the captain.

—Joseph Conrad, "The Secret Sharer"

T he short story is a form of literature that often has deeply ambiguous
qualities, much like the oceans. Short stories can be relatively brief or quite
long; choppy and fast-moving or set at a leisurely pace; brutally realistic
or sketched in a kind of magical realism, full of dreamy interludes. They can pass
a forgettable half an hour as a brief entertainment, or—like "Benito Cereno" by
Herman Melville—can easily withstand a lifetime of scrutiny and analysis. To me,
a good short story of the sea brings three essential elements together: first and most
obviously, a setting that has a good deal of salt water in it; second, a suspenseful
plot whose outcome is not easily guessed; and third, a message or lesson for the
attentive reader. It is hard to pack all that into a somewhat truncated format, but
some of the greatest writers in Western history have done so.

When I was constructing a syllabus for a literature of the sea course at Tufts University in the 1980s, I knew I wanted to include several short stories. Given the format of three class sessions each week, it was not unreasonable to ask the students to read a couple of longer form stories and use the week studying them in depth. Unlike a lengthy sea novel like *Moby-Dick* or Patrick O'Brian's *Post Captain*, the students could really sink their teeth into short stories. Fortunately for me, three professors at the U.S. Naval Academy in Annapolis had done a thorough survey of existing short stories of the sea and created a single volume (lengthy, at close to six hundred pages) that swept up all of the stories I wanted to assign.

Thus, I came on to *Short Stories of the Sea*, a book I cherish for the sheer sweep and scale of its choices.[1] Taken alongside the same authors' earlier compendium of sea poetry, these two books together can, in many ways, form the cornerstone of a sailor's literary bookshelf. The authors have organized the thirty-four stories into five sections, each of which is introduced by a brief essay. Of note, unlike the volume of sea poetry, *Short Stories of the Sea* benefits greatly from concise but incisive mini biographies of each of the contributing writers. The sections are "Sea and Shore," capturing the linkages between the oceans and those who seek to sail them or wait for those who do; "Sea Lore and Legend," which depicts some of the best "sea stories" that mariners spin as yarns between themselves; "Adventures at Sea," including some snapshots of ships in combat; and "Storm and Shipwreck," about the dangers posed by the sea that every captain faces in bringing his or her ship safe to harbor.

The final section is "Great Stories of the Sea," and here we find four lengthier short stories (some would call them novellas) that are the absolute apotheosis of this genre. Of all the stories of the sea I have ever read, the greatest is "The Secret Sharer" by Joseph Conrad. Prosaically, it tells the story of a captain in a small vessel who allows a stowaway to come on board and hides him in his cabin. Metaphorically, it is a meditation on command—the loneliness of being the captain, the tension within ourselves that must be overcome in command, and the ease with which the sea can cause us to subtly lose our bearings. As a former commanding officer at sea myself, several times over, I can attest to the challenges that each sea captain grapples with in managing his or her own "secret sharer"—your own innermost thoughts, hopes, and doubts.

Also in this section is a powerful short story by Herman Melville (author, of course, of *Moby-Dick*). Titled "Benito Cereno," the name of a ship, it describes a confident commanding officer who comes upon a vessel in distress and naturally seeks to aid it. But the captain quickly discovers that there is reason to pity the strangely acting crew of the ship, and as the mystery deepens, he fears the outcome. The ship is a slaver, and the tables have been turned—or so it comes to seem. Ultimately, it is a powerful story of racial injustice that could have been written for our times today. Alongside *Moby-Dick*, it is a crown jewel in the extensive oeuvre of Melville.

The final section also includes a small masterpiece, "The Life Boat," by Stephen Crane, author of *The Red Badge of Courage*. Here he grapples with the moral choices in front of four men drifting at sea in a lifeboat from the just-sunk steamer *Commodore*. The story begins with as good a description as I know of being on the deep ocean in a very small boat: "None of them knew the color of the sky. Their eyes glanced level and were fastened upon the waves that swept toward them. These waves were of the hue of slate, save for the tops, which were of foaming white, and all of the men knew the colors of the sea." Crane, who died prematurely at the age of twenty-eight, actually underwent a similar thirty-hour experience in a small dingy, and the story reflects the realism of his near-death event.

Also making appearances in these pages are writers as diverse as Nathaniel Hawthorne, Sarah Orne Jewett, John Masefield (also a superb poet), Somerset Maugham, F. Scott Fitzgerald, John Updike, Rudyard Kipling, Mark Twain, C. S. Forester (of "Hornblower" fame), Edgar Allan Poe, and Ernest Hemingway, among others. Perhaps the most inspirational story is by the author of the novel *The Cruel Sea*, Nicholas Monsarrat. The short story, titled "HMS Marlborough Will Enter Harbour," is about a ship whose stalwart captain is determined to make it safely to port after a near sinking in combat. Deeply moving, suspenseful, and nautically accurate, it offers an ultimately hopeful conclusion to a very difficult voyage.

Each of the stories in this collection is superbly told, ably introduced, and thematically important to understanding the oceans and our relationship to them. For a single volume with which to deeply understand the sea, *Short Stories of the Sea* sails closest to the wind of any book on this sailor's bookshelf.

CHAPTER THIRTY

THE BEDFORD INCIDENT

by Mark Rascovich

If he fires one, I'll fire one.

—Capt. Eric Finlander of USS *Bedford*[1]

O ne of the best and most dramatic movies I saw as a young boy was *The Bedford Incident*, which came out in 1965 as I was beginning my own personal journey to the sea. When I saw the movie's depiction of an American destroyer operating at the height of the Cold War in the waters off Greenland, I thought it was exciting and inspiring—even though (spoiler alert!) the ending was nearly apocalyptic to include a mushroom cloud at sea. I read the novel a few years later as a teenager, and it helped confirm my desire to attend the Naval Academy at Annapolis. Since those long-ago days, I have returned to the book many times, and over my desk at home hangs a framed cover of the first edition. It is the ultimate cautionary tale from a geopolitical standpoint, but the real power of this extraordinary tale set entirely at sea is the dangers of obsession in command.

The story begins as a U.S. journalist arrives on an advanced U.S. antisubmarine destroyer operating somewhere in the Greenland–Iceland–United Kingdom "gap" during the days of Soviet and U.S. at-sea "cat and mouse." A Soviet submarine, which metaphorically becomes the "great whale" of this Moby Dick–like narrative, is undetected. But the captain of *Bedford*, the hyper-efficient and utterly focused Eric Finlander, is doing all he can to harass the submarine. Because the sub has to surface from time to time, Finlander believes he can eventually force his prey to the surface and pin down its precise location—and enhance his chances of promotion to rear admiral. The American journalist, Ben Munceford, is a down-on-his-luck freelancer with a duffle bag of dirty clothes, a secondhand camera, and a divorce hanging over his head. The leitmotif of the novel is the reoccurring series of submarine detections as *Bedford* closes in.

The secondary characters include the newly arrived ship's doctor, who is concerned about the extreme tension he detects in the crew; an insecure young ensign trying hard to appease his demanding captain; and—strangely—a German commodore who is on board as a NATO representative. The portrait of Captain Finlander is harsh, depicting him as a somewhat abusive skipper who has only one thing he truly cares about and that is finding the submarine and humiliating its captain, his opposite number. Even the captain's surname, Finlander, has echoes of the Cold War and the occupation and "Finlandization" of anyone who would "go soft" on the Soviets.

By the time the submarine is forced into a watery corner by a lack of air and maneuver space, Finlander has targeted it with his "ASROC" (antisubmarine rocket) nuclear depth charges affixed to missiles. The crew is exhausted, but the captain feels himself fully in control of the situation. He then remarks to his team that he will not be the first to fire, but—in immortal Cold War words— "if he fires one, I'll fire one." The stressed young ensign mistakes the captain's intent and hears only "fire one." He does so, destroying the submarine, even as Finlander's promotion to rear admiral arrives on board. Realizing the magnitude of this action, the German commodore believes that if the Soviets learn of the destruction of their sub, they will be forced to respond and escalate the crisis to a potential global nuclear war. To prevent this, he climbs one of the ASROC missiles—observed from the bridge where the crew is powerless to stop him— and detonates one of the weapons. This causes *Bedford* to sink, thus evening the score between the United States and the Soviet Union. Improbably, the journalist survives the explosion and is picked up at the end of the novel—by a Russian trawler and the sub's so-called mother ship, the *Novo Sibirsk*, which is fruitlessly searching for the submarine.

The Bedford Incident is a classic of Cold War literature, much like *Seven Days in May* (about an attempted military coup in the United States) and *Fail-Safe* (in which the United States and Soviet Union trade strikes on major cities in order to avoid all-out war). It captures the tensions of the day and reflects several similar incidents in the 1960s, including one around the time of the 1962 Cuban missile crisis. But in terms of sea literature, this is a book about a mission-obsessed commanding officer and a tired, overworked, and ultimately mistake-prone crew. The lesson for any sea captain, or a landsman as well, is that in leadership you reap what you have sown. Captain Finlander is ambitious and drives his crew obsessively after a goal he believes his superiors want him to achieve. In so doing, he exhausts and demoralizes them to the point of making fatal errors.

The presence of a NATO commodore (and, ironically, a German one who had recently experienced firsthand the horrors of war on his own national soil), is a surprising plot twist. As is often the case in sea literature, there emerges someone on the ship (often a crewmember, but occasionally a passenger) who impacts the captain's complete control over his or her universe. Such turnabouts in narrative reflect the way in which the sea itself can change in an instant, and ultimately we must realize that we cannot control every situation. Captain Finlander learns the lesson too late to save himself and his crew, and together they pay the steepest of prices. The gain—avoiding a nuclear war—is a worthy one but could have been achieved without death and destruction had the captain taken a more rational approach to his mission.

Bonus: Reading *The Bedford Incident* alongside *Moby-Dick* is especially powerful, and I have grouped them side by side on my personal bookshelf. Both are stories of man's obsession at sea and of how events so often pass in the end to the endless ocean. Mark Rascovich closes his remarkable novel with the sight of Ben Munceford, the lone survivor of *Bedford* being rescued: "On the fourth hour, a ship drew near, nearer, and picked him up at last. It was the devious cruising Novo Sibirsk, who, in her retracing search after her missing children, found only another orphan."[2] The echoes of the ending of *Moby-Dick* and the strange tale of Ahab and the *Pequod* is reinforced in this classic novel.

CHAPTER THIRTY-ONE

THE CAINE MUTINY

by Herman Wouk

I'll tell you this, the same things seem goddamn
different in the middle of a typhoon when they're
happening, and six thousand miles away in the Federal
Office Building when you're talking about them.

—Lieutenant Maryk speaks to Lieutenant Greenwald, his
lawyer, as they first discuss the case.[1]

Herman Wouk, the author of *The Caine Mutiny*, lived to be 103 years old. He wrote many books, including the magisterial pair of novels that cover essentially all of World War II, *The Winds of War* and *War and Remembrance*. Everything he wrote is very good, but he will live forever in sea literature for his extraordinary novel about a rusty old destroyer mine-sweeper, a supremely difficult captain, a mixed bag of a wardroom, a horrific typhoon, and a nail-biting court-martial. The seagoing and combat portions of the novel are very realistic, reflecting Wouk's time in uniform on a similar class of ship in the Pacific during the same period. In a dense, complex, and compelling book of nearly five hundred pages, he teases out the complicated relationship between a commanding officer and his officers at sea better than any other single book I've read.

In my hand as I write this is a battered 1951 first edition of the novel, with a slightly tattered cover, which I treasure above almost any book in the five thousand volumes in my personal library. I picked it up for seven dollars at a used bookstore in the late 1960s, and it is worth many, many times that now. But its principal power hit me in reading it as I prepared to go to Annapolis in the 1970s, when it was recommended by a Navy lieutenant who had become a mentor to me in the process of applying. He said, "Queeg is the captain you don't want to be. But you don't want to be Keefer ether." The words meant nothing to me at the time, but over the years of my career, I've returned again and again to *The Caine Mutiny*, working hard not to be a failure *either* as a leader *or* as a follower. The lesson of this novel, which has become a kind of cartoon depiction of a twisted tyrant in command, is really about what both leaders and followers owe *each other*, especially in the demanding crucible of the sea.

Set at the height of World War II in the Pacific, the novel follows the voyage of a battered destroyer minesweeper through a series of combat operations and its near sinking in the real-world Typhoon Cobra in December 1944 (which destroyed and damaged numerous ships of the American Third Fleet off the Philippine islands). Told through the eyes of a young, naïve, privileged Princeton graduate, Willie Keith, it focuses on the command tour of Lt. Cdr. Philip Queeg, a stiff-neck regular Navy officer who believes he needs to "square away" the ship. His methods for doing so include severely browbeating the officers in the wardroom in a style of leadership that today would be described as "toxic." Queeg is a poor shiphandler and a worse tactician, whose behavior during combat off one of the islands being invaded in the campaign becomes a deep embarrassment for his wardroom, who increasingly criticize and scorn the captain.

The executive officer and second in command, Lt. Steve Maryk, falls under the intellectual sway of the sophisticated reservist Lt. Tom Keefer. Thus are sown the seeds of the mutiny by pointing out that Section 184 of Navy regulations allows a subordinate to take command if a commanding officer proves incompetent. The executive officer begins to keep a log of the captain's supposedly paranoid behavior, with an eye toward reporting it to the chain of command. Soon the ship is hammered in a massive typhoon (based on a different but also real 1945 storm that Wouk experienced firsthand on his ship). Queeg is paralyzed with fear, and Maryk relieves him, with support from Willie and the helmsman on the bridge. This scene is powerfully depicted and is as good a description of the stress and tension that descends on a ship's navigational bridge in a life-threatening storm as any in literature.

The real climax of the novel, however, is not at sea; but in a courtroom in San Francisco where the executive officer stands accused of mutiny. Until this point in the novel all the reader's sympathy is lodged with Maryk and the wardroom and against Queeg. But the backstory supplied by the court officers, especially the Jewish lieutenant, Greenwald, begins to introduce the complexity that makes this such a fine work of sea literature. Greenwald, who is acutely aware that people like Queeg and other regular military are the backbone of the U.S. defense capability (especially in the unrewarding interwar years), is actually disgusted with the "mutineers," and especially the slippery would-be novelist, Tom Keefer. Greenwald destroys Queeg on the stand and wins an acquittal for his client. But at the party afterward, he calls out Keefer, insults him, and challenges him to a fight—a challenge the cowardly Keefer declines. The choice of "*Caine*" for the name of the ship echoes the betrayals that go both ways and are illuminated at this powerful climax of the novel.

The final portions of the book bring the story full circle. Maryk, although acquitted, is career-terminated by the Navy. Ironically, Keefer becomes the captain of the *Caine* but behaves in a cowardly fashion himself and is especially ashamed because his brother (also in the Navy) dies in combat operations heroically. Young Willie (the Wouk of the novel, in many ways) comes of age and becomes "the last captain of the *Caine*," awarded a Bronze Star following combat operations *and* receiving a letter of reprimand for his role in the mutiny—reflecting the ambiguous outcomes of the story. As the ship heads for decommissioning and the war ends, the reader is left with a nagging sense that narrators can be unreliable, and outcomes never fit a preordained pattern. That is certainly the case for anyone who has been through a serious storm at sea, and the events of the mutiny and its aftermath form a sea story worth reading again and again.

Bonus: The 1954 film version is brilliant and was nominated for Best Picture at the Academy Awards. It alos earned Humphrey Bogart (Captain Queeg) a nomination for Best Actor, although the Oscar that year went to Marlon Brando for another watery picture, *On the Waterfront*. When the movie opens, a few lines cross the screen that say, "There has never been a mutiny in a ship of the United States Navy."[2]

CHAPTER THIRTY-TWO

THE CRUEL SEA

by Nicholas Monsarrat

The Captain carried them all. For him, there was
no fixed watch, no time set aside when he was
free to relax, and if he could, to sleep. He was strong,
calm, uncomplaining, and wonderfully dependable.
That was the sort of Captain to have.[1]

One could argue that the most important single book to the American naval profession has a simple and evocative title: *Command at Sea*. It is published today by the Naval Institute Press, the book-publishing arm of the United States Naval Institute, the professional organization of the sea services (Navy, Marine Corps, Coast Guard, Merchant Marine), and first appeared in 1943, written by Cap. Harley Cope and reflecting the vast World War II experience of the U.S. Navy.

It has since been through six editions, and I have had the honor to serve as editor on several of them, including the forthcoming seventh edition. Captain Cope begins the foreword to his first edition of this classic by saying, "Every young officer who is worth his salt looks forward eagerly to his first command, whether it be a destroyer, a minesweeper, a submarine, a PT, or an auxiliary." *Command at Sea* is the compilation of the seagoing wisdom of generations of American naval officers and represents the inherited customs, traditions, and seagoing attributes of the British Royal Navy.

At the beginning of the book—on the first page—in fact is a quote from *The Cruel Sea*, a novel by Nicholas Monsarrat published in 1951, which is atop this brief essay. It reflects the fictional Royal Navy captain of HMS *Compass Rose*. When I first set out to revise *Command at Sea*, I was struggling to shape a few words that could summarize what a sailor wants and expects from his or her commanding officer. I looked through Navy Regulations, of course, and many professional manuals. Finding nothing quite right, I began to reread many sea novels that place command at sea at the center of a powerful narrative—writers like Patrick O'Brian, Herman Wouk, Joseph Conrad, Rudyard Kipling, C. S. Forester came and went. But it was in *The Cruel Sea* that I found just the right evocation of that mix of reliability, resilience, and selflessness that for me personifies the servant captain at sea.

The novel is set largely at sea and occurs during the Battle of the Atlantic that in many ways shaped the outcome of World War II. The ships of the novel are small—corvettes and frigates—and the sea is vast and, indeed, cruel. The book starts in 1939 as the war is beginning. Each of the seven chapters covers a year in the war, and as the characters grow in experience and share in the small victories and larger tragedies of combat operations, they also come to recognize the importance of command and leadership in creating the conditions that make the harsh life of the sea in small combatants bearable.

Nicholas Monsarrat knew that life well, having come into the Royal Navy to serve in those same small ships, conducting dangerous escort duties. His wartime service included duty in the Flower-class corvettes and River-class frigates that are featured in *The Cruel Sea*. Although he was philosophically a pacifist, he was a sailor growing up and volunteered for the Royal Naval Volunteer Reserve near the beginning of the war. He rose through the officer ranks and ended the war a lieutenant commander and had command of three frigates. After the war he entered the British Foreign Service and was posted to Africa and Canada. He died in the late 1970s and was buried at sea by the Royal Navy. Every word he writes of the sea in his novels rings true, and like all experienced sailors, he has a love-hate relationship with the oceans.

The plot of the novel is quite simple. It revolves in large measure around the maturation of Lockhart, a young sub-lieutenant, and his captain, Lt. Cdr. George Ericson, who is recalled to duty and takes command of the HMS *Compass Rose*. In the ship, the initial first lieutenant is a bully and a poor officer, but he leaves the ship, and the remaining officers in the small wardroom settle into a wartime routine. Their duties include crossing the Atlantic again and again, in the stressful work of convoy duties. If the allies cannot maintain the vital open sea lanes of communication, Britain (and potentially Russia) are doomed to fall to the Nazis. The duty is unimaginably hard, especially in the small ships, which pitch and roll continuously. The crews were literally "walking on the walls" as they go about their routine business, punctuated by the attacks of the ever-lurking U-boats. I wrote about this in the *New York Times* in 2020.[2]

Eventually their luck runs out and the ship is torpedoed and sunk in 1943, with most of the crew dying of exposure in the freezing waters. The captain, Ericson, and two of the officers survive and are rescued, although one of Lockhart's fellow junior officers suffers a mental breakdown and is hospitalized. Ericson and Lockhart go to a fresh command, HMS *Saltash*, and survive the war together. A tragic backstory follows the wartime love affair of Lockhart with a young woman officer in the Women's Royal Naval Service, demonstrating even further the supreme cruelty of the sea—especially in war time.

As both a meditation on command and an illuminating story of the destructive power that emerges when the sea combines with war, *The Cruel Sea* will always be a classic of seagoing literature. Even for experienced mariners, the sheer length of time spent at sea and the brutal pressure of combat will shock. To understand the sacrifice of a sea captain in the worst of circumstances, this is the book to read.

Bonus: Another view of the Battle of the Atlantic in a more compressed form (just a day in the life of the captain) is *The Good Shepherd* by C. S. Forester, also included in *The Sailor's Bookshelf*.

CHAPTER
THIRTY-THREE

THE GOOD SHEPHERD

by C. S. Forester

A destroyer captain's duty was to build
as well as to destroy.[1]

*T*he *Good Shepherd* by C. S. Forester's has long held a special resonance for me, as I have been both a destroyer captain and then a commodore in charge of a group of destroyers in combat (like Commander Krause, the protagonist of this fine sea story). It was also published the year I was born, 1955, when memories of World War II, in which it is set, still burned bright. As a teenager I read many of the sea novels of C. S. Forester, particularly the Hornblower series, about a nineteenth-century British warship captain fighting in the Napoleonic era. I found them captivating, and they are still a good gateway for younger readers preparing to trade up to the vastly more complex and thought-provoking novels of Patrick O'Brian. I enjoyed the stories of Horatio Hornblower, but the C. S. Forester book I keep coming back to remains *The Good Shepherd*. It was part of the reason I became interested in Annapolis, and it inspired me to my first service selection coming out of the U.S. Naval Academy:

a brand-new *Spruance*-class destroyer, USS *Hewitt*. And further apropos of *The Good Shepherd*, which is about the cat-and-mouse battles of the North Atlantic between submarines and destroyers, my very first job in the Navy was as an anti-submarine warfare officer. So much of this taut, beautifully written story has resonated with me through decades in the Navy.

The story opens at the height of the Battle of the Atlantic, and the protagonist, Cdr. George Krause, is an Annapolis graduate in the midst of a frankly mediocre career as a surface warfare officer. Despite some shortfalls along the way and a failed marriage, Krause has achieved his heart's professional desire, command of a destroyer. His fictional command is the USS *Keeling*, a small 1,800-ton *Mahan*-class destroyer engaged in the bread-and-butter of destroyer operations in World War II: convoy protection. Without the ability to move troops and supplies from the United States to its European allies, the war effort against the Nazis would have quickly ground to a halt.

Realizing this, Hitler created a fearsome force of U-boats, diesel submarines with relatively high technology profiles for that day. The allies were forced into prolonged convoy operations and were working feverishly to create the necessary technological advances to beat the U-boats: sonars (which can track large metal objects underwater, like subs and torpedoes) and better radars that could be capable of detecting the slim profile of a periscope mast out of the water for only a limited time. Commander Krause's warship is modestly outfitted for such operations, and he is in charge of protecting a large convoy of merchant ships with only his own and three other allied warships—British, Canadian, and Polish. Interestingly, this is Commander Krause's first real combat experience, and the captains of the other warships, while junior to him in rank and under his authority, are much more experienced in convoy protection combat operations.

The writing, like all of C. S. Forester's, is immensely readable. You are plunged into the story in an instant, and everywhere around you the sound of the sea can be heard—in the harsh weather, the rocking of the ship underfoot, the distant smudges on the horizon that are the convoy ships, the signal lamps clattering back and forth with messages, and the sight and sounds associated with the appearance of the U-boats. The story only covers about two days at sea (around fifty hours), but it begins calmly enough with the captain emerging from his morning shower and preparing to shave. Before he can complete his morning ablutions, he is peremptorily summoned to the bridge by his watch officer because of a contact report from one of the allied ships. He is immediately faced with a difficult decision, the first of a long series of them that will intrude on his day: whether or not to detach two of the protecting warships to prosecute the tenuous contact. Krause gives permission and must adjust his position in the screen accordingly.

As the long day unfolds, we see his inner voice again and again on full display—without a chance for a break in the actions, he is challenged to make the right decision. His insecurities are high, as they would be for most captains (and certainly were for me) in similar situations. We see his mood swings, hear his biblical quotes (he is extremely religious), and eventually learn that he has been passed over for promotion, presumably because of the high degree of competition in the interwar Navy. He is acutely aware that he has been given this chance for command at sea by a divine providence, and he is hoping to make the most of it. Above all, we see a combat commander making the hardest of decisions on a minute-by-minute basis, knowing that his choices will have life-and-death consequences for the ships in the convoy and perhaps even for the warships under his command.

The book is notable for the purity and accuracy of the inner voice of the captain but also for its extended reflection on the sea itself. It opens with a beautiful passage: "In that hour after dawn the horizon did not seem far away. The line where the watery sky met the gray sea was not clearly defined; it was as if the cheerless clouds grew denser out towards that circle until at the final meeting, all the way round, there was not an abrupt transition, but a simple mingling of twin elements."[2] I have always felt that looking at the horizon from the bridge of a ship at sea, we are looking not at simple meteorological phenomena but rather are peering at eternity itself. Forester conveys that beautifully throughout this elegant novel.

In the end, Krause brings through thirty of the thirty-seven merchant ships that started the convoy with him, despite encountering a full-blown "wolf pack" of multiple U-boats. He loses one of the escorting destroyers but in turn has sunk two U-boats and perhaps a third. Commended by the relieving commodore, he collapses on his bunk, the sea rocking him to a deep and untroubled sleep. As Forester says, "The long gray rollers from the northeast swept in endless succession across the area, each demonstrating its unlimited power." By the end of *The Good Shepherd*, our captain has indeed earned his rest.

Bonus: The recent film *Greyhound*, which stars Tom Hanks in the role of Commander Krause, was inspired by *The Good Shepherd* and is outstanding and highly accurate. Only ninety minutes in length, it continues the superb work of Hanks in showing war realistically to the audience, as he also did with particular brilliance in *Saving Private Ryan*.

CHAPTER THIRTY-FOUR

LIFE OF PI

by Yann Martel

The ship sank. It made a sound like a
monstrous metallic burp. Things bubbled at
the surface and then vanished. Everything was
screaming: the sea, the wind, my heart.[1]

I have always loved magical realism in the world of literature. This is a strain of fiction writing in which things exist in a novel or short story (or even a poem) that cannot quite be squared with the real world. The most famous writer of magical realism, who is especially prominent in the literature of Latin America, is the Nobel Prize–winner Gabriel García Márquez. His extraordinary novel *One Hundred Years of Solitude* is widely regarded as the classic example of modern magical realism. Some other authors who deal in this style of writing include Toni Morrison (*Beloved*), Salman Rushdie (*Midnight's Children*), Haruki Murakami (*1Q84*), Günter Grass (*The Tin Drum*), and Neil Gaiman (*The Ocean at the End of the Lane*). In such novels there are often ghostly visitations, dreamlike sequences, mythological gods, talking animals, imagined events, and unreliable narrators.

Frankly, there is very little magical realism in sea literature, although there are a few examples. Edgar Allan Poe's only fully developed nineteenth-century novel, *The Narrative of Arthur Gordon Pym of Nantucket*, has some of these characteristics. "The Rime of the Ancient Mariner," an epic poem written in 1797–98 by Samuel Taylor Coleridge, likewise explores this course, with, for example, a scene in which "Death" and "Nightmare Life in Death" (a woman) appear on board and play dice for the souls of the crew. The illustrations for the poem done by Gustave Doré are stunning, deeply evocative, and unsettling. Of the handful of sea works of literature that venture into this style, *Life of Pi* is by far the best. It is allegorical, mysterious, full of highly sentient animals, and centers around a 227-day ordeal in a lifeboat by a survivor from a terrible shipwreck in the Pacific Ocean and an adult Bengal tiger. What could be better?

The book was published by Knopf initially in Canada (Yann Martel is Canadian) and, after being rejected by many publishing houses, won the Man Booker Prize in 2002. It has sold millions of copies worldwide and been published in dozens of languages. The Ang Lee film, released in 2012, was likewise a major hit around the world and was nominated for eleven Academy Awards, winning four, including Best Director. Although only about half the book is set at sea, the thematic events are all driven by the dynamics of lifeboat survival, which is a fundamental part of sea literature. Martel explores codes of survival, cannibalism, hierarchic command, and resilience at sea—he just happens to use a cast of characters that includes a very competitive group of animals and a young man fighting his fears and inadequacies to dominate and survive.

The story opens in India, where the narrator, Piscine Molitor Patel, lives as the son of a zookeeper. His name, which means "swimming pool" in French, is shortened to simply "Pi" when he starts high school. Pi becomes aware of a massive Bengal tiger named "Richard Parker"—an homage to Poe's Pym novel, mentioned above, by the way. The first part of the novel ends when the family, along with animals from the zoo, take a ship bound for Canada in the mid-1970s when Pi is sixteen years old. The doomed Japanese freighter *Tsimtsum* sinks, and Pi manages to escape to a small lifeboat. Unfortunately for him, the boat holds a hyena, a zebra, and an orangutan, who begin killing each other. As the hyena eyes Pi for his next meal, the Bengal tiger Richard Parker emerges from under a tarp and kills the hyena.

With the two of them now alone in the lifeboat, Pi begins to try to dominate the big cat using a combination of food as a carrot and seasickness as a stick. This creates an uneasy balance in the boat, and various other adventures ensue including encounters with another castaway, a network of algae with thousands of small meerkats, and encounters with sea creatures.

Eventually, after 227 days, the lifeboat comes ashore on the Mexican coast. Without a backward glance, Richard Parker saunters into the jungle and disappears. The brief final part of the book is the "investigation" conducted by Japanese officials who understandably find the initial recounting of events utterly implausible. As Pi presents alternate explanations for the events, he eventually convinces them of the version with the animals, concluding this odd, improbable, but highly metaphorical novel.

Martel's parable can be given several interpretations and explanations, and each reader will bring his or her own life experiences to the story of Pi. For me, this is a novel about the implacable forces that we face in life, especially at sea. The animals Pi faces are to some degree the variety of fears that he must overcome, and the huge, lurking tiger, Richard Parker—who saves his life and then abandons him—could be imagined to be courage, resilience, and the power we find within ourselves in the most challenging circumstances. It could also be a manifestation of God and faith, which can both challenge us and save us or abandon us as life moves on. One could also see Richard Parker as the sea, summoning the best of us, then receding from our consciousness as we come ashore. As Martel's Pi says early in his ordeal, "I must say a word about fear. It is life's only true opponent. Only fear can defeat life. It is a clever, treacherous adversary, how well I know."[2]

Suffused throughout the book is a deep appreciation of both the beauty and danger of the sea: "The storm came on slowly one afternoon. The clouds looked as if they were stumbling along before the wind, frightened. The sea took its cue. It started rising and falling in a manner that made my heart sink. What I had seen up to now were mere hillocks of water. These swells were truly mountains. Climbing the giant swells, the boat clung to the sea anchors like a mountain climber to a rope."[3] As Pi learns to survive in the lifeboat (aided by a handy cache of survival gear), his self-confidence grows.

As the book concludes, after the lifeboat washes ashore, Japanese investigators submit a brief report on the sinking of the vessel. The investigators summarize by saying, "Very few castaways can claim to have survived so long at sea as Mr. Patel, and none in the company of an adult Bengal tiger." Magical realism indeed, but a fine sea story to be sure.

Bonus: The 2012 film is a worthy accompaniment, as is Poe's novel, *The Narrative of Arthur Gordon Pym of Nantucket.*

CHAPTER THIRTY-FIVE

THE OLD MAN AND THE SEA

by Ernest Hemingway

Then the fish came alive, with his death in him, and rose
high out of the water showing all his great length and
width and all his power and his beauty. He seemed to hang
in the air above the old man in the skiff. Then he fell into
the water with a crash that sent spray over the old man and
over all of the skiff.[1]

I have always loved the novels of Ernest Hemingway, which I began to read in the late 1960s as a young teenager. The lean style of the prose, born of a newspaper reporter's training that started Hemingway as a writer, reminded me of the sea—clean and fresh on the surface, and yet full of hidden depth and meaning beneath. He wrote many brilliant novels, of course, including *The Sun Also Rises*, *A Farewell to Arms*, *Islands in the Stream*, and *To Have and Have Not*. Many of them include scenes set at sea, often with a star turn for some version of his beloved boat, *Pilar*. Hemingway loved to hunt on safari, watch bullfights, ski at a breakneck pace, drink hard, and chase women—but, above all, he loved the sea and fishing. It is therefore quite appropriate that what many consider his final capstone work is a short novella set almost entirely on the ocean, *The Old Man and the Sea*. It was the last significant piece of writing published by Hemingway before his suicide in 1961. The book won a Pulitzer Prize in 1953 and led directly to his winning the Nobel Prize for literature in 1954.

Hemingway follows the travails and ultimate defeat of a Cuban fisherman named Santiago. The old man is toward the end of his life but still strong and vital. He loves baseball, the sea, and even the fish he seeks to catch, saying, "It is good that we do not have to try to kill the sun or the moon or the stars. It is enough to live on the sea and kill our true brothers."[2] As the story opens, Santiago is living in a small shack on the beach, scraping by on little food, no money, and old newspapers in which he can follow the pro baseball leagues in the United States, albeit weeks after the fact. He has gone eighty-four long days without catching a serious fish, and the parents of his young apprentice, Manolin, have insisted that the boy sign on instead with a luckier boat. Still, the young apprentice is loyal to Santiago and tries to help him prepare his gear and sail well out into the Gulf Stream to break his unlucky streak the next day.

On that eighty-fifth day Santiago does indeed sail into deep waters of the Gulf Stream (a natural phenomenon that always fascinated Hemingway, with powerful warm waters full of sea life). He quickly hooks a big marlin, perhaps the largest he has ever seen, and the great fish takes him on a long ride across the waters of the stream for two nights and three days. Santiago says again how much he loves and respects the fish, which in many ways is a metaphor for the struggle of life itself. On the third day, Santiago lands the great fish, stabbing him with a boat hook. But at this point in the struggle, as is so often the case in life at moments of deep crisis and seeming triumph, Santiago is exhausted but fulfilled. He heads home in his skiff, the marlin strapped to the side of his small craft because it is too big to haul in fully.

But on the voyage home, the blood of the marlin sends an irresistible call to the many sharks in the warm waters of the Gulf. Santiago kills one, a big mako, but loses his harpoon in the process. With a makeshift harpoon forged from a knife, he continues to battle to stop the many sharks that continue to feed on the corpse of the marlin. While he kills a handful, and drives away more, by morning the marlin is essentially a skeleton still strapped to the side of the boat. All that is left is the head, tail, and vertebrae. Santiago knows he is defeated, and all his strength is gone. Yet he manages to make it to shore and falls asleep in his shack.

The next day, the other fishermen gather around the skiff and see that the marlin is among the largest fish ever caught in the village. They realize what has happened, and when a tourist wanders over and inquires, the fisherman says in Spanish, "Tiberon," or shark. The tourists believe it is a shark, a symbol of the uncaring and naïve society that cannot understand the epic struggle of a lone man with the sea.

The true first edition of *The Old Man and the Sea* is the September 1, 1952, issue of the old *Look* magazine, which ran the story in its entirety and sold 5 million copies. The first edition print run was also enormous for the 1950s, at 50,000 copies. I have both editions, and often pick up the small hardcover volume, especially when I am trying to think through a challenging moment in my life. There are certainly varying literary analyses of the meaning of Santiago's struggle, defeat, and resilience. For me, it is a book about exactly what the title says: a man and the sea. It is an old man because, as he wrote it, Hemingway thought of himself as old and grizzled (he was in his mid-fifties, by the way, although much battered physically and mentally by this point in his life), the "Papa Hemingway" of society pages. But Hemingway also believed in the ability to overcome challenges, saying poignantly on the subject of resilience: "But man is not made for defeat. A man can be destroyed but not defeated" and "the world breaks everyone, and afterward, some are strong at the broken places."[3] The lessons I take away from the story of Santiago are exactly that: in the end, we are all defeated and broken in some way, but we can choose to dream and fight on.

As a sea novel, the book succeeds brilliantly. It is also a meditation on the profession of fishing, something Hemingway deeply respected. His descriptions of being on the deep ocean in a very small boat, fighting the massive fish that dominate those waters, will resonate for anyone seeking to understand the challenges of the sea. Santiago, like Hemingway himself, is an immortal character—and one tied inextricably to the sea.

Bonus: The 1958 film, starring Spencer Tracy as Santiago, was nominated for several Academy Awards, including Best Actor. The music and photography are noteworthy, and at only eighty-seven minutes, this is a short, tight masterpiece.

SAILORS IN NONFICTION

CHAPTER THIRTY-SIX

TURNER & THE SEA

by Christine Riding and Richard Johns

It is only when we are no longer fearful
that we begin to create.

—J. M. W. Turner

T here are many powerful and important painters whose work illuminates the sea and man's relationship to the oceans. But none is more associated with the production of art that has immediacy and centrality to the story of the sea than Joseph Mallord William Turner. Throughout my many years at sea, I usually traveled with a set of watercolors and turned out truly mediocre (at best) paintings, usually of the sea, coastlines, and other ships. From time to time I would gift my poor offerings to fellow officers, who, stifling an inner sigh I am sure, would accept them. My painting has never improved, despite considerable attention and effort. Such is life. But whenever I wanted inspiration or an approach to follow in the world of sea art, I turned to J. M. W. Turner. The very best of the hundreds of books of his work that I have found is *Turner & the Sea*, published in 2013 by Thames & Hudson and produced in conjunction with the truly exceptional Peabody Essex Museum in Salem, Massachusetts. It was there that I came across the book, and the museum is the ideal location to highlight such an important artist, his work, and quality literature like this. The book itself is gorgeous, an oversized coffee-table volume with 225 images, many double-page spreads of Turner's most important works. Each page is a delight and the text tells the story of Turner, his times, and his voyage as a sea painter.

Turner was born in 1775 in London and came from decidedly middle-class (at best) roots. As is so often the case with artistic talent, it manifested early and, happily, his parents encouraged it. He began as a draftsman and architectural painter and early on caught the eye of important English art critics. Turner exhibited early, starting in 1791, in watercolor. His early oil paintings began to emerge toward the very end of the 1700s. Over time he painted simple seascapes, epic battle scenes, shipwrecks and storms, the coastal regions, rivers and estuaries, sunrises and sunsets over the oceans—essentially any subject involving the seas and rivers of the earth. He studied and was an associate at the Royal Academy of Arts, and his circle of patrons (and purchasers) steadily grew in the early 1800s.

His career took off during the years of the Napoleonic Wars between France and essentially the rest of Europe. Given the heroic efforts of the Royal Navy in that period (serving in ships that were the "wooden walls" that protected England), there was keen interest among the public in sea painting. During the brief Peace of Amiens in 1802, Turner was able to visit the Continent and the Louvre in Paris. All of the first four decades of his life essentially had a backdrop of war at sea, given that the final defeat of Napoleon did not occur until the Battle of Waterloo in 1815. Some of Turner's best-known works reflected this, including two of my personal favorites, *The Battle of Trafalgar* and *The* Victory [Lord Nelson's flagship at Trafalgar] *Returning from Trafalgar*. The former is perhaps the most famous of his naval paintings, and the extraordinary sweep of the scene is remarkable. It is a massive oil that combines a number of elements from the battle: a falling mast (perhaps to represent the death of Vice Admiral Nelson in the battle); code flags spelling out the famous d-u-t-y message that every man must do his duty for England; the French warship *Redoubtable*, which sank in a storm after the battle; and a mix of Spanish and French warships behind the massive form of *Victory*.

In the foreground of the painting are a mass of ordinary sailors who have fallen overboard but managed to make their way to longboats. The overall scene is one of chaos, heroism, death, and destruction—with a beautifully realized patina of patriotism shining through.

Turner was a difficult man to like. He was deeply private and never married (although he had two daughters with his housekeeper). He famously said, "I hate married men. They never make any sacrifices to the arts, but are always thinking of their duties to their wives and families or some rubbish of that sort."[1] The word "eccentric" comes to mind, although I prefer to think that, like the sea, he simply became more unpredictable as he aged; he became even stranger, and this unsettled personality gradually entered into his art. Although still beautiful, his work became more melancholy and reflective as he neared the end of a relatively long (for that period) life of seventy-six years. One of his most evocative paintings seemed to be a symbol for the way life will wear us all down in the end, like the sea wears down the shells that wash ashore: *The Fighting termeraire tugged to her last Berth to be broken up.* The painting, an oil of medium size, shows one of the truly distinguished warships at Trafalgar being unceremoniously pulled up the Thames by a steam tug. The ship is contrasted with a symbolic setting sun and seems also to connote the passing of the age of sail and a certain ambiguous view of the power of British sea power.

In addition to his brilliant work in oils, J. M. W. Turner will always be known as a superb watercolorist. I can tell you from personal experience that painting with watercolor is very difficult; unlike oil, which simply sticks to the canvas (and can be scraped away in the case of mistakes), watercolor runs and saturates the paper, cannot be redone once applied (only painted over, leading to a mushy appearance), and is notoriously difficult to manage in terms of color on the finished page. Yet it is the perfect medium to paint the sea, which is constantly changing and shifting in tone and color. Turner's watercolors are, to my eye, the very best of his work.

In *Turner & the Sea*, Christine Riding and Richard Johns (and other contributors) have done a spectacular job not only of capturing the legacy of one of the premier artists of the nineteenth century but of getting down in one beautifully illustrated volume the way in which art can bring the sea to life for us all.

Bonus: One of my other favorite sea painters passed away several years ago, but his work is easily available: Ian Marshall. Trained as an architect, he painted all manner of sea scenes but specialized in ships—especially warships. Some of his best books of art include *Passage East* (with John Maxtone-Graham) and *Cruisers and La Guerre de Course.*

CHAPTER
THIRTY-SEVEN

THE AUTOBIOGRAPHY
OF GEORGE DEWEY
Admiral of the United States Navy and
Hero of the Spanish-American War

by George Dewey with Frederick Palmer

You may fire when ready, Gridley.

—Admiral Dewey to his flag captain embarked in USS
Olympia at the Battle of Manila Bay, 1898

I n the preface to this superb 1913 autobiography of one of our nation's greatest naval officers, Admiral of the Navy George Dewey starts with two simple sentences: "It was my fortune to be in command on May 1, 1898, of an
American squadron in the first important naval action against a foreign foe since
the War of 1812. The morning that we steamed into Manila Bay marked an epoch
in the history of our navy and in that of our country in its relations with other
great nations."[1] The book covers more than sixty years in the long life of George

Dewey, from his youth in Vermont through the act of Congress that kept him on active duty for all the remaining years of his life, ending as an "Admiral of the Navy," a rank only he has ever held. The historical sweep of the life of our nation, including the Civil War, the opening of the Pacific, and the acquisition of overseas colonies, is captured in this memoir set against the backdrop of long years of sea duty.

My own associations with the admiral are relatively recent. In May 2018, I was asked to give the graduation address at Norwich University in Vermont. At the time I was the dean of The Fletcher School of Law and Diplomacy at Tufts University and several years into my post-Navy life. I'd given several commencement speeches previously and enjoyed the format. The real challenges of such speeches are keeping the remarks short, the students awake, and the faculty mildly interested. Avoiding bromides and platitudes is key (never say "reach for the stars," "all you have to do is dream it," or "be kind to others"). Equally important is maintaining humility and a sense of humor. A real plus is having a local hook, something that shows the assembled crowd that you've done your homework and "get" the culture and history of the school.

The oldest private military college in the United States, Norwich University was founded in 1819—before West Point, Annapolis, the Citadel, or the Virginia Military Institute. In a typical year, it has more than four thousand students and a vibrant corps of cadets who are commissioned into all the different services. Located in the tiny town of Northfield, Vermont, it is a long way from the sea and predictably has produced a succession of stalwart Army officers (including well over a hundred generals) through its two-hundred-year history. As I began my search for a suitable "hook," I was quite surprised to discover that the highest-ranking officer ever to pass through Norwich was not a general but an admiral. And not just any admiral, either, but the only formally designated lifelong "Admiral of the Navy" in American history: George Dewey, victor of the lopsided Battle of Manila Bay against Spain in 1898.

Up to that point I had had only a passing knowledge of George Dewey as the answer to the trivia question, "Who is the highest-ranking officer in the history of the Navy?" And of course I had learned the basics of the Battle of Manila Bay where, as commander of the U.S. Asiatic Fleet, Dewey calmly ordered his forces into the battle with the simple order to his flag captain, "You may fire when ready, Gridley." But the more I researched the life of this sixty-two-year veteran of the Navy, who began his career fighting in the Civil War and ended his service with an accurate (though controversial) prediction of a coming war with Germany, the more I became fascinated by him. In the speech at Norwich, I wanted to make Dewey come alive for the audience and draw some life lessons for the graduating cadets and the rest of the student body.

I began my research of Dewey with this immensely readable autobiography, which captures his steady, calm, and resolute voice across the nearly two centuries, going back to his birth in 1837. In terms of tone and sobriety it reads quite a bit like the classic memoirs of President Ulysses S. Grant, felt by many to be the best military memoir in American history. Dewey's volume has that kind of restrained pace and honesty to it and is in a sense a seagoing version of Grant, set in the mid- to late nineteenth century. While he glosses over a few less than perfect moments in his long career (see the skeptical *Admiral of the New Empire: The Life and Career of George Dewey* by Ronald Spector), overall, it reads to me as direct and honest personal history, with plenty of salt water.

I discovered to my surprise that Dewey was a true hellion in his youth, someone who repeatedly bucked authority, got into serious fights, and had several brushes with the law. As a result, his father shipped him off to a military school, thinking it would instill some discipline in this wild child. That school, of course, was Norwich. Although not fully explained in the autobiography, there are reports that he was expelled from Norwich for "drunkenness and herding sheep into the barracks." That experience was apparently not an impediment for his subsequent enrollment in the Naval Academy, which also claims him, but Dewey's experiences at Norwich helped shape him and lead inexorably to that moment on Manila Bay. All of this is sketched out in the autobiography, although admittedly seen from the great distance of older-age and post-Navy retirement.

In many ways, he was *not* an extraordinary junior or midgrade officer, although he had some memorable moments on the Mississippi during the Civil War over the days of the extensive blockade that eventually choked off the Southern states. There was a sense of normalcy about him, and few would have predicted he would ascend to the absolute heights of the naval service. For example, in the years between the Civil War and what he called "the Spanish War," he served two years as a lighthouse inspector and four years as naval secretary of the lighthouse board—hardly a pair of glamorous assignments, and the reader can feel his sense of absence from the sea.[2]

But Dewey was brave, thorough, and—having gotten his temper under control—began to rise steadily if not spectacularly through the ranks. It is important to remember that he was also a deep admirer of Adm. David Farragut and, indeed, fought under him in several notable Civil War battles on the Mississippi.[3] Yet he continued to have a rough streak that would emerge in certain circumstances. One biographer said he had a "lifelong pattern of striking first and filling out forms later."[4] As the book unfolds, the reader truly feels the influence of sea duty on Dewey. While not a poetic writer, he captures his feelings about the importance of the oceans in America's strategic vision. He also includes many personal anecdotes about his time in command, sailing on distant seas including his eventual posting to the far Pacific.

By the time he reached flag rank, Dewey had well and truly settled himself and earned the friendship (and political influence) of Theodore Roosevelt and several other up-and-comers in Washington. Dewey's appointment to command of the Asiatic Fleet fulfilled a lifelong dream to lead a squadron in forward operations— and happened just in time to get a call to action against the Spanish colonies in the Pacific. His decision to sail immediately for Manila Bay, stretch his logistic chain to its absolute breaking point, and disregard the possibility of mines in the vast harbor in order to strike hard and fast at the Spanish fleet is worth examining closely—and holds some parallel lessons with the decision of his mentor Farragut at Mobile Bay. It is also a story that captures the vast distances of the Pacific and the way that the inexorable space of the oceans directly influences the seagoing decisions of any mariner.

Dewey's was a fascinating and distinctly American naval life, and I was amazed I had not spent more time getting to know the Admiral of the Navy better while I was still on active duty. Thinking back on my own forward deployments as a combat commander—with vastly more firepower under my command—I wish I had known more about this turn-of-the-last-century admiral. His ethos and sensibility would have helped inform my own decisions in the turbulent twenty-first century. Reading his autobiography is a distinct window into America in the nineteenth century at sea, a coming-of-age story about an early American naval officer, and a journey to sea with a seasoned mariner. It richly deserves a place in this sailor's library.

Bonus: Ronald Spector's somewhat critical analysis of Dewey provides a balance to the admiral's self-assessments. *Admiral of the New Empire: The Life and Career of George Dewey* was published by Viking Press in 2001 and is well worth the read alongside the autobiography.

CHAPTER THIRTY-EIGHT

EMPIRES OF THE SEA
The Siege of Malta, the Battle of Lepanto, and the Contest for the Center of the World

by Roger Crowley

The day drew to its mournful close; the bloody water, heaving thickly with the matted debris of the battle, reddened in the sunset. Burning hulks flared in the dark, smoking and ruined. The wind got up.[1]

As I sat down a few years ago to write *Sea Power: The History and Geopolitics of the World's Oceans*, I knew I would have to comment on the most meaningful naval battles in history. Sadly, there are an almost infinite number to choose from, covering all the vast oceans of the world. Certainly, the ancient Greek–Persian conflict of 2,500 years ago at the Bay of Salamis makes the list. The Roman–Egyptian battle at Actium as well. Any British admiral would say Lord Nelson's triumph at the Battle of Trafalgar, where he destroyed the combined Spanish-French fleets of Napoleon, was the key naval battle of all

146

time. Most American admirals like me would highlight the triumph of admirals Chester Nimitz and Ray Spruance at Midway, turning the tide of World War II. I think there are an additional handful of other conflicts that occurred along the long voyage of the past three thousand years of human history at sea that matter deeply. But of them all, the most historically impactful sea battle may be the lesser-known Battle of Lepanto in 1571. Roger Crowley's brilliant and extremely readable history *Empires of the Sea* certainly makes that case.

I invited Roger to NATO to give a talk about the book, which is really "Geopolitics 101" at sea. He readily agreed and gave a bravura presentation that resonated well with my team. In the book, Crowley begins by quickly sketching out the two centuries leading up to the battle. During the Crusades, the Mediterranean served as a springboard for the Christian zealots of Europe to push their way into the Holy Land; and the newly (and relatively briefly) established "Crusader kingdoms" depended on the seas for resupply, logistics, and trade. The Crusades also gave great impetus to the rise of Venice and the Italian commercial cities over the course of the 250 years of various Christian campaigns. Venice was particularly well positioned in the northern Adriatic, with easy access to the trade coming from Europe over the Alps and superb, relatively safe access to the Mediterranean itself.

As Crowley clearly illuminates in the book, the Venetians were clever geopolitical actors indeed—rather than seeking to hold huge swaths of territory (with all the attendant headaches of administration), they sought a series of trading bases. They acquired Crete and Cyprus, two of the most strategically positioned islands of the Mediterranean. They also built smaller forts and trading stations around the periphery of the Eastern Mediterranean. In a way, they anticipated—by some six centuries—Alfred Thayer Mahan, the father of modern sea power strategy, in systematically building commercial and trading stations strategically around their world. Crowley, by the way, has written in more depth about Venice in his excellent 2011 book, *City of Fortune: How Venice Ruled the Seas.*

All of this was militarily anchored by the great Arsenal of Venice, which was an early-technology assembly-line construction facility producing great galleys. The Venetians used seagoing technology cleverly and at one time had a fleet of thousands of ships and tens of thousands of seamen—despite only having a core population of around 200,000 souls. Their relationships with other kingdoms and empires were based largely on trade, and they were adept at playing off the Christian rulers against each other and manipulating them with the power of the Church and the control offered by the papacy. They seemed destined to dominate the Eastern Mediterranean and were growing richer and richer—all due to geopolitical planning, excellent use of geography in the region, and the application of new technologies in construction, weaponry, and administration.

Crowley begins his tale in earnest with the fall of Constantinople in the mid-1400s as the Venetians and the rest of Christian Europe are on a collision course with the rising power of the Islamic Ottomans. After taking Constantinople, the Ottomans were able to push into Europe on land as far as Vienna and to increasingly dominate large tracts of strategic seacoasts along the eastern and southern Mediterranean. Their practices were brutal, even by the standards of the day, and included forced conversions to Islam, slavery, and a particular focus on capturing Christian ships and enslaving their crews. The two civilizations—Christian and Muslim—were on a collision course that would bring great strife throughout the 1500s and 1600s.

As with previous conflicts in the Mediterranean, geography played an important role. The Ottomans were able to use their sea bases along the coasts and sought to reach out into the island chains of the Aegean and to the west. The Europeans tried to use the coastal bases of Italy as their strategic bastion while attempting to dominate the same strategic islands. Technologies—cannon, sail, rowing, marine tactics—were roughly equal, although the Ottomans had a better system of administration and training in that it was relatively uniform throughout their growing empire. The Christian west had a collection of different systems at play, which made it more difficult for them to operate seamlessly when fleets from different national entities came together.

Crowley renders in great detail the fall of the strategically important island of Cyprus in the Eastern Mediterranean to the Ottomans in 1570. It was an epic siege that ended tragically for the Christian defenders. This alarmed the various competing European nations to the point that the pope formed an "anti-Muslim League," principally backed and manned by the Italians and the Spanish. The Turks continued to push both on land and at sea, and soon it was clear that a significant sea battle would decide the directions of the maritime campaign and in many ways determine the fate of Europe. That battle occurred near Lepanto, on the western side of what is today the Dalmatian coast of the Adriatic Sea.

Crowley makes readers feel as though they are under way in the glittering waters of the Mediterranean. The day of the battle dawned clear and bright: October 7, 1571. The Turks brought over 250 galleys manned by 75,000 seamen and soldiers; and the allied European fleet, commanded by the Austrian prince Don Juan, was made up of roughly two hundred galleys manned by slightly over 70,000 seamen and rowers. Crucially, the Venetians provided a half dozen galleasses—big, heavy, floating forts with terrible killing power. This would be the first great galley battle since Actium, some sixteen centuries earlier and in roughly the same part of the Mediterranean. Notably, the Ottomans came to it with overwhelming confidence, not having lost a significant sea battle in over a century.

But by the time the battle ended around 4 p.m., the sea was literally red with blood—almost all of it Ottoman. The Turks lost the vast majority of their ships, escaping with fewer than fifty vessels at a cost of over 25,000 skilled seaman and marines. The Christian forces lost but 7,000 men and a dozen ships. It was a day upon which history turned, and it marked the high-water level of Ottoman maritime ambitions for the broader Mediterranean. It was the Romans who called the Mediterranean "the center of the world," and the Battle of Lepanto ensured it would remain largely in Christian hands.[2] The difference was tactical acumen by the Europeans, especially in the use of the galleasses, which forced the Turks to maneuver around them and sustain heavy losses from their large cannon. Almost all the fighting occurred hand to hand, and the commanders were personally involved, with Don John leading the assault that ended up killing his opposite number.

The battle was incredibly decisive in the moment, preventing the further expansion of Islam into the Christian world, but—luckily for the Turks—the lack of follow-up by the Christian powers allowed the moment to pass without a significant loss of territory by the Ottomans. The Christians quickly reverted to form with bickering and arguing that allowed the Turks to hold Cyprus, and their ships continued to rove the Mediterranean in force. Despite the setback of Lepanto, the Turks rebuilt their fleet, worked hard to retrain a sailing force, and continued to be a factor in the Eastern Mediterranean, where they skirmished with the forces of Italy and Spain for much of the next two centuries. But they never again truly threatened to fully dominate the entire "inner sea" of the Mediterranean, which was at one point a realistic ambition for them.

Their failure at Lepanto meant that the Ottoman Empire, as powerful as it would become and as long as it would last, would be bounded. They would not push past the deserts of Arabia to the south, past the Persians to the east, or past the Europeans at sea and in the Balkans to the west. Perhaps most importantly coming out of the Battle of Lepanto, the mortal fear of the "invincible Turks" felt by many southern Europeans was shattered. In that important sense, it was a critically important battle.

When I was the NATO commander, I went often to Spain, a country I love for many reasons—from the beauty of the language and culture to the excellence of the cuisine to the deep sense of history on the Iberian Peninsula. It is a place that was once an uneasy part of the Islamic world, and the architecture, language, and culture of parts of southern Spain—such as Seville—greatly reflect this. At one of the military summits we held in Seville, my Spanish counterpart presented me with a beautifully decorated bottle of Spanish brandy in a hand-painted box. The motif on the box was representation of the Battle of Lepanto, replete with a blood-red sea and the Spanish and Italian flags flying over the victorious Christian fleets. It is a Mediterranean sea battle that changed history across the Mediterranean, from the Aegean and the Adriatic all the way to the Strait of Gibraltar, by shutting the door to further Ottoman expansion into the central and western Mediterranean.

For a sailor to read *Empires of the Sea* is to almost feel the ships under way and hear the sails snapping in the breeze. You can smell the gunpowder and hear the crack of cannons over the waves and wind. Crowley focuses on the geopolitics as backdrop, but the great strength of this book is a realistic focus on war at sea. It includes descriptions of the sea battles and sieges against the islands of Cyprus and Malta as well as the more or less constant activities of pirates. The centerpiece, of course, is Lepanto, and there is not a better description written. The entire book is truly an engrossing read, and one that keeps the reader's sensibilities under way with every page.

Bonus: *Venice,* by Jan Morris, is short, historically accurate, and illustrates the power of the city-state-empire throughout the middle ages in crisp, readable prose. It is a nice fit with *Empires of the Sea,* as is, of course, Roger Crowley's 2011 book about Venice mentioned above, *City of Fortune.*

CHAPTER THIRTY-NINE

IN THE HEART OF THE SEA
The Tragedy of the Whaleship *Essex*

by Nathaniel Philbrick

To the last I grapple with thee; from hell's heart I stab at
thee; for hate's sake I spit my last breath at thee.

—Captain Ahab to the white whale[1]

I first met Nat Philbrick, the author of *In the Heart of the Sea*, at a dinner party in Boston when I was dean at The Fletcher School at Tufts. He is a life-long racing sailor who has won many prizes and championships at sea and was cordially surprised to discover (at my own admission) that I am not a very accomplished sailor (as in one who can handle a small boat with sails). I pointed out I was sort of a "power-boat sailor," and he laughed and asked me the size the biggest ship I'd "skippered." I allowed that would be either a 9,000-ton destroyer of some 505 feet in length or, depending on how you define command, a nuclear-powered aircraft carrier (in my case the 100,000-ton *Enterprise*, with eight reactors and over 1,100 feet in length). We clinked wine glasses to "command at sea, whatever the size of the vessel" and have been good friends since then.

At that time he had already published a nice brace of books about events at sea, including *In the Heart of the Sea*, which won the National Book Award for nonfiction in 2000. At the dinner party he told me he was working on a book about the Battle of Yorktown (a Revolutionary War combined-arms fight combining both land and sea forces of the United States and France against Great Britain). Over the years I have read most of his other books and have in my collection signed first editions of five of them. But the one I keep coming back to, and recommending to others with real passion, is *In the Heart of the Sea*. I love the book for its narrative drive, the way Philbrick gently connects the events with the fictional story of Moby Dick, and, above all, for his beautifully nuanced and realistic portrayal of life at sea—both in relatively calm sailing and of course in true crisis.

The story opens in Nantucket, the (at the time) isolated island off the coast of Massachusetts and at one time one of the wealthiest locations in the country because of its principal industry, whaling. It then follows the final ill-starred two-year voyage of whaleship *Essex*, which sails down the Atlantic Ocean, crosses at the Cape of Good Hope, and ends up in the Pacific. The story is told through the eyes of two of the ship's crew: the arrogant and unrepentant first mate, Owen Chase, and a fourteen-year-old cabin boy, Thomas Nickerson. The stories provide a "full spectrum" view of the cruise, a disastrous encounter with the whale that sinks their ship, and the harrowing events afterward.

In many ways, the book echoes *Moby-Dick*, beginning with the crew ashore and describing the fascinating and unique life of the whaling community ashore in the early 1800s. It then follows the crew closely as they head to sea in *Essex*, including along the way a great deal of technical information about the really astounding profession of whaling: "First the mates hacked a hole in the whale's side, just above the fin, into which was inserted a giant hook suspended from the mast. Next the mates cut out the start of a five foot wide strip of blubber adjacent to the hook. Pulled by the tackle attached to the windlass, the strip was gradually torn from the whale's carcass, slowly spinning it around, until a twenty foot long strip, dripping with blood and oil suspended from the rigging."

By November *Essex* was well into its voyage when it is attacked by an enraged sperm whale in the deep Pacific. This was an event beyond the ken of Capt.

George Pollard and his crew as no other such attack had ever been reported. Indeed, when it finally became known as survivors made it home, it shook the whaling industry and became, of course, the basis for the novel *Moby-Dick*. After *Essex* is destroyed, the crew take to the longboats, and—fearful of cannibals (irony alert) on the Marquesas, which were "only 1,000 miles away" and downwind—decide to attempt to sail east to the coast of South America. This is a voyage over two thousand miles and upwind, and it was a decision taken with arrogance and probably false information.

The journey east has all the terrible experiences you could imagine—a roasting tropical sun alternating with difficult seas, deadly challenges to command in an unimaginable scenario, starvation and dehydration, and eventually cannibalization—the fate that kept them away from the vastly easier voyage to the Marquesas. This included cannibalizing those that died a "natural" death in the small boats, and eventually required the drawing of lots for another victim—who turned out to be the captain's young cousin. Melville spent time with the surviving mate, and then spun a novel that will live forever. The irony of Melville's *Moby-Dick*, of course, is that the *Pequod* is lost with all hands, excepting only Ishmael, the narrator, who is rescued. The torment of the crew of the *Essex*, largely self-inflicted, actually begins in earnest when they man the lifeboats.

There are many, many powerful books about sailors cast adrift in lifeboats and rafts on the deep ocean and somehow surviving, but this is the most memorable account I've read. Nat Philbrick has written a masterpiece that stands adjacent to the "great American novel" by Melville, and the two fine works are of a piece in terms of quality and impact on how we think about the sea.

Bonus: *In Search of Moby Dick: The Quest for the White Whale*, by Tim Severin, takes the reader through the waters of the central Pacific, from the Philippines to Indonesia and much of Micronesia.[2] He searches among those communities for another Moby Dick, a story of a killer whale. It is a search that connects the nineteenth and twentieth centuries and fits neatly with both the novel *Moby-Dick* and Nathaniel Philbrick's story of the *Essex*.

CHAPTER FORTY

LADY IN THE NAVY
A Personal Reminiscence

by Joy Bright Hancock

And so, when the legislation was finally enacted, a call for women's services was issued. There was not draft or conscription involved, but the women came forward, eagerly and proudly, to contribute their talents and skills.[1]

The life of Joy Bright Hancock was exciting, meaningful, and full of service to her nation. She was born in 1898 in New Jersey and lived a long life that revolved around her devotion to the U.S. Navy and the maritime capabilities of the United States. Her memoir, *Lady in the Navy*, is beautifully written, and in many ways serves as an anthem for the slow, difficult advancement of women at sea. As a U.S. Navy veteran of both World War I and World War II, she was instrumental in the rise of the WAVES (Women Accepted for Volunteer Emergency Service), one of the very first women officers in the history of the Navy and the commander of nearly seven thousand women at the peak of the WAVES program.

The book is quite personal for me because when I was the captain of USS *Barry*, the second of the *Arleigh Burke*–class destroyers, the Navy unexpectedly and suddenly selected my warship to be the first of the class to have women join the crew. Heretofore in my career, I'd had very little contact with women in the Navy: I was part of the last Annapolis class to graduate before any women were admitted as midshipmen; all of my ships had all-male crews; and even on shore duty, there simply were very few women in any significant roles. Now, suddenly, I was going to lead a mixed-gender crew to sea. So I turned to books and history to learn about the role of women in the Navy, and one of the first things I read was Joy Bright's captivating, honest, and frankly, quite entertaining memoir.

She enlisted in the Navy during World War I after a stint in business school in Philadelphia and served as a yeoman (essentially an office worker) during the war. The photograph on the cover of this autobiography shows her in the uniform of the day, with a petty officer's crow on her sleeve, and she eventually rose to become a yeoman first class and chief yeoman of the Cape May Naval Air Station. After the war she continued an affiliation with the Navy by working at the Bureau of Aeronautics, founding a magazine about naval aviation. She was married twice in the interwar period and, tragically and astoundingly, both of her husbands—young, heroic naval aviators—were killed in aviation mishaps involving airships, then in their infancy. Her first husband, Lt. Charles Gray Little, died in 1921 (when she was just twenty-three years old). Of his death in a terrible explosion in an experimental airship, she said, "In recollection, the months which followed seem formless. Still many things had to be done and life had to be lived."[2]

She remarried three years later, in 1924, to Lt. Cdr. Lewis Hancock, who died just over a year later in another airship crash in September 1925. It is hard to imagine the sorrow she must have felt in her mid-twenties; after the loss of her second husband, she was incapacitated for nearly a year in hospital. Fortunately, she recovered her health—and promptly went to sea, going with her sister on an around-the-world cruise. After visiting the seaports of the East, she said, "This trip was my introduction to filth, disease, famine, dust and heat as well as indescribable beauty, for Asia is a continent of overwhelming contrasts."[3]

After sailing the world and subsequently learning to fly, saying—logically enough after losing two husbands in aviation accidents—"I reasoned that if I learned to fly, I might conquer my fear of it."[4] After World War II broke out, she volunteered and was commissioned in the WAVES, ascending steadily in rank so that by the end of the war, she was a commander and in charge of all WAVES. As the third director of the WAVES, she was central to the Women's Armed Services Integration Act of 1948, which integrated women directly into the naval service. This was a crucial step toward truly opening the Navy to women, and she was repeatedly recognized for her efforts in gender integration, eventually leading to women pilots and seagoing deck officers.[5]

Her final promotion, to captain after only six years of commissioned service, was among the speediest in U.S. Navy history. Her story continued throughout the post–World War II period, and Captain Hancock guided the WAVES through an initial contraction and eventually an expansion that brought them into the regular Navy, rather than being in some special category of reservists. This was the most important contribution of her long and distinguished career, and you can drop a plumb line from her work to the cadre of women who joined USS *Barry* in the mid-1990s. That plumb line continues today, with the full opening of all rates, ranks, and ships to women in the Navy, and the contributions women four-star admirals like my good friend Michelle Howard have made in their careers.

In the mid-1950s she was married a third time, to a naval aviator she had known as a junior officer in the 1920s, now a vice admiral, Ralph Ofstie, a highly decorated officer in World War II and the Korean War. He was selected for command of the Sixth Fleet in Europe, and they spent their first year of marriage there in the port-to-port schedule of a busy flag officer. Tragically, he contracted cancer and died in 1956 after only two years of marriage.

Joy Bright Hancock knew much personal sadness in her life, losing three husbands—all naval officers—but it never affected her brisk, energetic, and determined voyage. While her days at sea may not have been many, her utter devotion to the Navy and thus to the sea is memorable. Reading this memoir allows you to sail in company of a true pioneering Navy officer who paved the way for generations of women officers who sailed in her wake.

CHAPTER FORTY-ONE

ONE HUNDRED DAYS
The Memoirs of the Falklands Battle Group Commander

by Adm. Sandy Woodward with Patrick Robinson

He takes us into the heart of fierce actions fought by the Royal Navy both in Falkland Sound and on the high seas.[1]

—Margaret Thatcher, prime minister of Great Britain

V ery few admirals in history have found themselves fighting at the far end of such a long supply chain as then–rear admiral Sandy Woodward, commander of the British task force sent into the deep Atlantic in the spring of 1982. After Argentina invaded the Falklands, a British overseas territory in the south Atlantic about 1,200 miles from Argentina (which claimed them) and 2,300 miles north of Antarctica, the government of Prime Minister Margaret Thatcher took the controversial decision of sending forces to retake the small, economically unimportant islands—as a matter of principle. The Argentines, who had gambled that the British would not want to risk blood and treasure to recapture islands where the sheep vastly outnumbered the people, badly misjudged the Brits. Only three days following the April 2 invasion, a British task force of twenty-five warships led by the carriers *Hermes* and *Invincible* were under way and headed south.

In a short, sharp war that lasted just under eighty days, the British retook the islands. The casualties were high for a six-week war: 255 Brits and 649 Argentines died. Most startling to many in navies around the world were the number of British warships sunk by Argentine long-range air: two destroyers, two frigates, a landing ship, a container ship, and a landing craft. The Argentine navy lost a cruiser, *Belgrano*, sunk by a British nuclear-powered submarine, as well as a diesel sub, four cargo vessels, two patrol boats, and a trawler. The loss of aircraft was similarly high, with the British losing thirty-four helicopters and fighters, and the Argentines nearly one hundred aircraft of all types.

At the time the war was fought, I was a young Navy lieutenant far from sea duty—I was midway through a two-year graduate program in international relations and law at The Fletcher School of Law and Diplomacy at Tufts University. Much, much later in life I would return after retiring from the Navy and become the dean there. I will always associate my time at Fletcher with the Falklands War, which was of course of considerable professional interest—especially to me as a surface warfare officer.

I followed the news closely, analyzing the results of each day's operations. It was clear, even from the far side of the world in Boston, that things in the south Atlantic were going to be a very "near-run thing" for the British if they were to succeed. They had no logistic base nearby, so everything depended on the flight decks of the two small aircraft carriers they had (each less than a third the size of a U.S. nuclear carrier). If one of the flight decks had been knocked out, it would have been game over because the remaining surface ships would not have combat air patrol aircraft overhead to help protect them from Argentine air.

Fortunately for the British, they had a very, very good commander, Sandy Woodward. He did not write his memoirs until nearly a decade after the events described in *One Hundred Days*, but when the book appeared, it became an instant classic of the profession and an in-depth, personal, and utterly candid depiction of war at sea in a tight, confined battlespace. Prime Minister Thatcher described Woodward as a "tall, rather stern, former nuclear submarine commander [who] sailed to the south with the highest academic and practical qualifications—in naval strategy and operations, nuclear engineering, anti-aircraft missile defense systems, computer technology, and senior naval planning and management techniques. There were those who considered him the cleverest man in the Navy. French newspapers called him 'Nelson.' "[2]

This modern-day Nelson shared several qualities with his distinguished predecessor (other than height, for Nelson was but five foot, six inches tall, compared to Woodward's towering stature). Like Nelson, Woodward favored simple and direct tactics; understood the importance of logistics to be ready for battle; had deep resilience in the face of losses in his force; and cared for each and every one of his sailors deeply. We know all this because of the high quality of the writing in *One Hundred Days*, which lets us sail hour-by-hour alongside the commander. We see Woodward's frustration and lack of sleep, sense his deep sympathy for the captains whose ships were literally shot out from under them, and come to understand his ability to synthesize the combat situation and take appropriate levels of risk with his dangerously extended force. In a chapter titled "The Bells of Hell," he writes, "Truth is generally recognized to be the first casualty of war, the second is almost certainly politeness. After just one day in battle, I now know the third. Sleep. A commodity rapidly becoming as rare as the first two. I replaced it, largely, with adrenalin."[3]

The entire British naval force eventually included almost 130 ships (43 warships; the rest auxiliary and merchants) and thousands of seamen, royal marines, and airmen. Operating weeks' sailing time from the closest base, Ascension Island off the coast of Africa, the force had to constantly contend with the gathering winter weather. Seas were building, temperatures dropping, and Admiral Woodward was very mindful of time shortening. "The weather now held us back badly, with great seas, poor visibility, rain, and wind. For three days we had not seen the sun."[4] Knowing the time pressure, he kept reminding himself that "ships are just as vulnerable as the marching armies of Napoleon and Hitler were in Russia. Everything goes wrong more often at sea when the weather is especially bad."[5]

The British were ultimately able to prevail in what became the most pitched battle at sea since World War II. It took a combination of British resilience, a rock-steady commander in Woodward, more than a pinch of luck, and—above all—an appreciation and understanding of the sea itself, a quality woven into the long strands of British naval DNA over centuries of seafaring. For a powerful memoir of modern combat at sea, *One Hundred Days* is the top of my list.

Bonus: After Admiral Woodward's masterpiece, the best broad-view book of the conflict is by veteran journalist and military historian Max Hastings, along with Simon Jenkins: *The Battle for the Falklands*, published in 1984. I've known Max for more than a decade, and he focuses like a laser on the Falklands war at sea, bringing both a journalist's attention to detail alongside a historian's sense of context and analysis.

CHAPTER FORTY-TWO

SEA OF THUNDER
Four Commanders and the Last
Great Naval Campaign, 1941–1945

by Evan Thomas

Where is Task Force Thirty Four repeat where is Task Force
Thirty Four RR the world wonders

—Naval message to Admiral Halsey[1]

In selecting a cornerstone book about the naval war in the Pacific during World War II, there were many volumes to choose from. For pure length, I could have gone with Samuel Eliot Morison's treatment of the Pacific portion of the conflict from his magisterial fifteen-volume opus, *History of United States Naval Operations in World War II*. Another good choice would have been famed naval historian Craig L. Symonds's single-volume *World War II at Sea: A Global History*, which came out in 2018. Certainly, another contender would be the 1963 edited effort by E. B. Potter and Fleet Admiral Chester Nimitz, *Triumph in the Pacific: The Navy's Struggle against Japan*. And there are many others.

But the book I kept coming back to and chose as most deserving a place on *The Sailor's Bookshelf* is *not* by a naval officer or a professional naval historian (although the author writes crackling good history and is a meticulous researcher). The book I chose is the marvelous *Sea of Thunder* by journalist Evan Thomas. The subtitle covers the structure—it's a look at the war in the Pacific through the actions and attitudes of four commanders: Adm. William "Bull" Halsey, a swaggering (and deeply racist) commander of the American fleet for much of the combat; the elegant Japanese admiral Takeo Kurita, a battleship force commander who launched a near-suicidal attack on the American forces poised to retake the Philippine Islands; another Japanese admiral, Matome Ugaki, who saw himself as the purest of samurai and led the kamikaze forces at the end of the war; and—the most appealing of the four—the relatively junior Navy commander Ernest Evans, captain in USS *Johnston*, a small destroyer that undertook a deeply heroic attack on a far larger Japanese force. Their stories collide at the biggest naval battle ever fought, the storied Battle of Leyte Gulf in October 1944.

In the course of telling the story of the battle, Thomas takes the reader through the vast U.S. maritime strategy to reconquer the Pacific Ocean and its hundreds of atolls, islands, barrier reefs, and littoral nations after the Japanese offensive wave of conquest had swept over much of it in the early days of the war. In outlining the strategy from both the U.S. and Japanese perspective, we see the immense stress placed on the commanders. Halsey has a variety of medical problems that may have contributed to his flawed decision in the battle that almost led to an American disaster. Halsey elected to send his entire force northward to take on Japanese forces, leaving the critical San Bernardino Strait unguarded. What's worse, he failed to inform his superiors—leading them to send the message that opens this chapter. The portrait of Halsey is a balanced and fair one, and hardly hagiography. But despite his flaws and missteps, especially his rash decision to take the striking power of his fleet north at a crucial moment, he comes off in the book as he was: a consummate sailor and an inspirational leader. As Thomas says, "Halsey had become the nation's admiral, the embodiment of American energy and can-do-ism, a bit reckless and crude, to be sure, but dominating and lionhearted."[2]

We see the increasingly desperate Japanese leaders who watch the noose built by America's vastly superior resources and industrial capacity tightening immutably around the Japanese home islands. As the game heads toward its almost inevitable conclusion, the tactics become more and more about dying with "honor" for the "glory" of the emperor and less about any real possibility of winning the war they started at Pearl Harbor. At the end, Ugaki led the final kamikaze raid himself, and took twenty-two junior officers with him. The last photo of him is in the book, with an enigmatic half-smile on his face.[3] Kurita, on the other hand, saw the futility of what was coming and survived the war, "unwilling to sacrifice his men in a futile gesture of nobility." At his funeral in 1978 he was praised as a "seaman of seamen."[4]

Most movingly, Thomas shifts the frame of observation from the high-level strategy and the admiral's decisions in the Flag mess to the deck plates of a small U.S. combatant and its well-led and plucky crew. The *Johnston* becomes one of a tiny handful of American surface combatants available to protect the landing force from the massive guns of the Japanese fleet closing on them after Halsey's blunder leaves them almost unguarded. With incredible courage, Captain Evans and his crew charge at and torpedo a Japanese heavy cruiser but then are sunk themselves and end up in the tropical waters with packs of sharks closing in.

Captain Evans would ultimately be awarded the Medal of Honor, and I know of few stories of valor that can top his tale of courage under fire "above and beyond the call of duty." A proud Native American of half-Cherokee and one-quarter Creek blood, his actions led to a far-superior Japanese force aborting their attack against the American forces about to land under Gen. Douglas MacArthur. In the waters off Samar in the Philippines, his torpedo attacks, smoke screens, and direction of supporting air bombardment bluffed the Japanese into thinking the landing force was better protected than it was in reality. Evans ultimately went down with his ship, having been severely wounded in the attack. According to Evan Thomas, after talking to one of Halsey's sailors who survived the battle, "Evans might as well have been John Paul Jones, personally aiming a 9-pounder cannon at the British from the ravaged quarterdeck of the *Bonhomme Richard* a century and a half before."[5]

By the conclusion of the book, we have attained a window into the four commanders that reflects the qualities and characteristics of naval officers well: the striking impulsiveness and determination of Halsey; the willfulness and utter devotion of Ugaki; the thoughtfulness and ultimate pragmatism of Kurita; and the pride and raw courage of Evans. In this great sea battle, this "sea of thunder," we can see qualities of leadership in command at sea on full display—with all the attendant flaws as well. Evan Thomas has written a fine book that tells the story of four sailors in the dark heart of a monumental battle at sea.

Bonus: The well-named book *The Last Stand of the Tin Can Sailors: The Extraordinary World War II Story of the U.S. Navy's Finest Hour* by a terrific naval historian, the late James Hornfischer, came out in 2004 to great acclaim. It focuses on the actions of *Johnston* and the other escorts in what some have called "the greatest upset in naval history."

CHAPTER FORTY-THREE

SHE CAPTAINS
Heroines and Hellions of the Sea

by Joan Druett

Preferring not to starve, Mary Read shifted back into men's
attire and shipped on a voyage to the West Indies.[1]

T he book *She Captains* is full of wonderful sea stories about women
who have gone to sea over the long centuries and how they have fared.
In today's world—where we have four-star women Navy admirals, female
captains of massive cruise ships and merchant bulk carriers, and even long-line
swordfish captains like Linda Greenlaw (see *The Hungry Sea* on this list)—some
of this sounds a bit quaint. But Joan Druett does a marvelous job simply telling
story after story about the bold female sailors who populate history.

Druett begins 2,500 years ago on the Volga river, telling the legendary story
of Queen Tomyris of the Massagetae, a river and Black Sea tribe fighting the
Persian Empire. According to legend, this "water woman" led her people to a significant victory in which the Persian emperor, Cyrus, was killed—and she then
searched for his corpse on the field of battle and cut off his head as a trophy. In

this tale we also meet the Amazons and sea nymphs of ancient Greek mythology, then move on to another great sea battle off the coast of Athens in the Bay of Salamis. At Salamis, Queen Artemisia of Halicarnassus (the home city of historian Herodotus) was leading a small force of five triremes as party of the Persian fleet (there were hundreds of the triremes on both sides). Although she advised the Persian emperor at that time, Xerxes, to avoid an Athenian maritime trap, she still fought on his side in the battle on September 23, 480 BC. According to Herodotus, she avoided death and escaped with her ships to fight another day.

Moving on to Rome and Egypt in the latter days of the Roman Republic, we encounter the legendary Cleopatra. Both Julius Caesar and Marc Antony fell under her spell, and she was at sea with the Egyptian warships under her command when Octavian broke the Roman-Egyptian fleet at the Battle of Actium. Well over a thousand ships fought in the battle, which was won by Agrippa, the admiral in command of Octavian's fleet. Like Salamis, Actium was a pivotal battle in ancient history, and both are still studied at Annapolis—see E. B. Potter's classic *Sea Power*, also one of our fifty books. Both Cleopatra and Artemisia were worthy female commanders from well over two millennia ago.

What next? The Vikings ravaged England in the years before and after 1000 AD and were noted for their extreme brutality. Among them were the "Valkyria," female Vikings whose ethos was based on the mythological handmaids of Odin, who sailed and fought alongside men. Notable among them was the rover queen, Alfhild, "who preferred a life of valor to one of ease. [She sought] to equal, or even to surpass male courage in the practice of piracy."[2] Alfhild's exploits are substantiated by a number of historians and included command of her own longboat and the completion of many successful raids. Other Norse women participated in both sailing the longboats and fighting ashore.

Later, as the "golden age of piracy" unfolds, we find women again and again involved in sailing, fighting, and pillaging. The Irish rover Grace "Grania" O'Malley commanded two hundred fighting men and three galleys operating out of Connacht in western Ireland. Descended from Gaelic nobility, she was a skilled seafarer in the mid-1500s. Her galleys were relatively small (rowed by thirty oars, plus sails) and carried about a hundred raiders each. By all accounts, she was a "resolute and reckless Admiral."[3] Her raids targeted merchant shipping heading to England, and she was able to acquire rich cargoes of wine, silk, silver, and gold. She remains an admired figure in Ireland today and was clearly a highly capable ship handler and warrior queen.

By the time piracy moved from the shores of England into the Caribbean, women pirates were operating as contemporaries of the notorious Bluebeard and Capt. John "Calico Jack" Rackham (reputedly the model for the fictional Capt. Jack Sparrow). We meet Mary Read and Anne Bonny, both accused (accurately) of piracy, which they conducted under threat of capture and execution in the 1700s. They have lived on in literature, a kind of watery Thelma and Louise, with fascinating backstories of personal tragedy, pregnancy, arrest and trial, and incarceration under brutal conditions. Both disappear from history around 1720 but live on in art, verse, and legend.

Druett includes a long section on the women of Vice Admiral Lord Nelson (notably, his winsome mistress Emma Hamilton) as well as cleverly written sections on the women embarked on board the "hen frigates" of the 1800s and 1900s. These were commercial ships (and occasionally warships) in which women were embarked as wives or lovers to members of the crew. Sometimes this happened quite openly, but there is much in the book about cross-dressing and the "deceit of dress."

A final story is about Betsey Miller, who was a mariner deeply involved in her father's shipping business in the mid-1800s. A newspaper article of the day said, "Amongst the fleet lately wind bound in Lamlash not the least but perhaps the greatest wonder was the good old brig Cloetus of Saltcoast, which for more than twenty years has been commanded by an heroic and exceedingly clever young lady, Miss Betsey Miller." As the article says, "she has weathered the storms of the deep when many commanders of the other sex have been driven to pieces on the rocks."[4] Her full story—quite remarkable—is well told in this fine book.

Taken together, the marvelously entertaining stories in this slim volume remind us of the role women have played over the years at sea. In today's world, we see women in every aspect of the maritime world, of course. When I commanded the guided missile destroyer USS *Barry*, I was proud to have a mixed-gender crew, and the women collectively were easily equal to and often better than the men. But today's female sea captains truly stand on the shoulders of those who have gone long before—as admirals, merchant sea captains, helmsmen and ordinary sailors, pirates, and navigators—"she-farers" stretching back 2,500 years. It is a story well worth knowing in the context of the journey of the human race to the oceans, and *She Captains* tells it well.

CHAPTER FORTY-FOUR

THE BATTLE OF SALAMIS
The Naval Encounter that Saved Greece— and Western Civilization

by Barry Strauss

Tomorrow, you must row for freedom.

—Adm. James Stavridis, speech, quoting Themistocles

W hen I was eight years old, my father, a colonel in the U.S. Marine Corps, was posted to Athens, Greece, as the assistant naval atta-ché. He was chosen mostly because he was a first-generation Greek American and fluent in the language. In preparation for our move, he began to tell me the stories of Greek mythology—Zeus, Hera, Poseidon, Ares, Athena, Apollo, Artemis, on and on. When we worked through the mythology, we turned to Greek history. The four great battles of the Persian-Greek wars were the canon, and thus I learned of Marathon, Thermopylae (scene of the famous fight of the three hundred Spartans), Plataea, and the single great sea battle, Salamis. I had a small set of models of triremes, the great rowed warships of those times 2,500 years ago, and I would set up the models in the dirt behind our house in the Athens suburbs, scratch out the shorelines of the Bay of Salamis near Athens, and array the fleet. The Greeks won the battle decisively, blunting the assault of Xerxes and putting an end finally to the episodic Persian invasions. Had they not won the battle, by the way, I might be writing this book in Farsi. Salamis was truly one of the "hinge battles" in history, where a different outcome would conceivably have produced vast ripples.

I have written elsewhere about Themistocles, the brilliant Greek admiral who commanded the Greek warships in the battle and his clever strategy.[1] Although I first heard of him in the early 1960s, over the course of my career I would often call on him as a model in crafting speeches about resilience and inspirational speaking.

I gave a speech in New York one Memorial Day as a four-star admiral on board the warship museum *Intrepid*. My remarks centered around his oration, which deeply inspired his mariners before the battle. He had a tragic ending to his life, eventually ending up exiled from Athens and becoming part of the court of the Persian kings. But he will live forever in the annals of naval history for his outstanding command of a vastly outnumbered Greek force (perhaps seven to one) that trounced the Persian fleet.

Since I have always been an immense fan of the Battle of Salamis, I invited the author of *The Battle of Salamis*, Professor Barry Strauss, to come and lecture to my team when I was Supreme Allied Commander at NATO around 2010.[2] Barry is a smart, gracious, and deeply credible authority on the ancient Greeks, and I was thrilled when he accepted our invitation. His talk about the battle was everything I hoped for: full of erudite observations about the technology of the warships on both sides of the battle; clever analysis of the importance of the admiralship, especially by Themistocles, who Strauss seemed to know almost personally; and—above all—the authority with which he unpacked the importance of the sea itself on the battle. As he spoke, you could almost feel yourself rowing at the oars, slicing through the Aegean Sea, watching the rough sail raise to help, and hearing the shouts of fellow mariners in the excitement of battle to come. Although I had been studying and thinking about the Battle of Salamis for almost half a century at that point in my life, his book illuminated the battle in a new and dramatic light.

Professor Strauss lives in Ithaca, New York, where he is professor of history and classics at Cornell University and a former chair of the department there. His expertise on the military history of the ancient world is extremely broad, ranging from ancient Greece, of course, to Rome, Persia, and Egypt. Among his many books in addition to *The Battle of Salamis* are such classics as *The Trojan War: A New History*, *The Spartacus War*, and—most recently—*Ten Caesars: Roman Emperors from Augustus to Constantine*. Strauss is himself an avid rower, and another of my favorite books by him is *Rowing against the Current: On Learning to Scull at Forty*, published roughly twenty years ago. I was interested to learn of his rowing prowess because his treatment of the Battle of Salamis has a deep appreciation for the act of rowing (the principal method of propulsion for the triremes) and the view the water's surface.

Salamis is not only a bay southeast of Athens but also an island. The battle was fought in 480 BC, and Professor Strauss's style puts the reader in the center of the action. The battle was delayed by the heroic efforts of the Spartan land force (the legendary three hundred Spartans and some other Greek allies) at Thermopylae. We meet various characters in the heart of the battle, such as Aminias, captain of the leading Greek warship. His personality and background are initially revealed; then we see him in the larger context of the fight. Similarly, we meet Artemisia of Caria, a queen of the Halicarnassus people, who perhaps was the first woman admiral in history. Similarly, we meet her early and then see her role in the battle on the side of the Persian king.

Strauss also helps readers navigate the understandably conflicting versions of the battle that have been handed down over the centuries. He helps us under-stand the Persian point of view, which is generally quite obscured by the fog not only of war but also of history itself. As he says, "Persia was neither deca-dent nor dull but a formidable and innovative power from which the ancient Greeks—and the modern West—borrowed much."[3] Understanding the Persians helps us understand the choices they made in the preparation for the sea battle and, indeed, why Themistocles ended up in their court after his rejection from Athens. Finally, Professor Strauss certainly lays out a good fight scene. After sev-eral initial forays by both sides, the battle eventually was fought in narrow straits between the island of Salamis and the mainland as a result of the Greek tactic of subterfuge—providing false intelligence to the enemy. The Persians were tricked into fighting in the narrows, where the advantage of their massive over-match in ship numbers was less of a factor.

After the battle, the Corinthians erected a monument engraved with the words, "When all Greece was balanced on the razor's edge; we protected her with our souls, and here we lie."[4] The Greeks went to sea and saved their world—and thus ours. This is their story, and it fits well on *The Sailor's Bookshelf*.

Bonus: Two films, *300* (2004) and *300: Rise of an Empire* (2014), are hardly credible history but are both watchable and at times moving, especially the first. The former focuses on the battle of Thermopylae and the glorious battle and tragic defeat of the three hundred Spartans, while the "sequel" is about the sea battles of Artemisium and Salamis. They are only loosely based on events and filmed in an interesting style that blends graphic novel presentation (from which *300* sprang) and real actors. Eva Green's performance in the latter film is notable for her passion and energy as she depicts the first true woman admiral in known history.

CHAPTER FORTY-FIVE

THE INFLUENCE OF SEA POWER UPON HISTORY, 1660–1783

by Alfred Thayer Mahan

Build me a thousand ships and I will give you the world.

—Euron Greyjoy, sea rover and ambitious
nobleman in *Game of Thrones*

My curious relationship with Rear Adm. Alfred Thayer Mahan began in 1972, when, as a first-year midshipman, I was herded with 1,200 of my new best friends into Mahan Hall at the U.S. Naval Academy to hear a lecture on sea power as part of our class indoctrination to the Navy.[1] I noticed a portrait of the grizzled, bald, mustachioed admiral in the foyer of the building. Despite the nineteenth-century naval uniform, he certainly looked every inch like what he was: an intellectual. Fyodor Dostoyevsky said that an intellectual was "a man with spectacles on his nose and winter in his heart." That would, in many ways, sum up Mahan, whom we would call today a national security policy wonk or a defense expert.

He was first and foremost a historian and a scholar. While he accomplished the minimum number of modestly successful seagoing assignments to earn promotions, his heart was almost entirely on the intellectual side of the Navy. His classic books about sea power, history, and geopolitics helped shape the course of his country's emergence as a global power, and Mahan's work in the early days of the U.S. Naval Institute—the professional organization of the U.S. Navy, Marine Corps, Coast Guard, and Merchant Marine—resonates today. In the end, Mahan's most important command was not a ship but the Naval War College; his work there continues to help chart a geostrategic course for America a century and a half after his departure. Mahan shaped our understanding of the seas.

Over the next four years as a midshipman, studying both engineering and English, I learned a lot more about Mahan and returned many times to Mahan Hall for lectures, performances (it is the home of the Naval Academy's troupe of midshipmen actors, known as the "Masqueraders," believe it or not), and debates. I started to develop my own belief that part of being a professional naval officer included an obligation to read, think, write, and—eventually—publish. Throughout my time at Annapolis, I would often sit down to write a column for the alumni magazine, *Shipmate*; an essay for the Academy's monthly literary magazine, *The Log*; or a short piece for *Proceedings*, the magazine of record for the sea services published by the Naval Institute that Mahan helped to shape early on. My classmates thought it strange that I would want to write and publish (especially the latter), but I continued to believe it is through being part of a larger conversation in a profession that we can best advance the interests of our community. Mahan was the beginning of all that for me personally and helped me think intellectually about the vitality and importance of the world oceans.

I had the honor of serving as the chair of the board of the U.S. Naval Institute from 2013 to 2019. During those six years, in my office in Beach Hall, the Institute's headquarters on the grounds of the Naval Academy, I had a sweeping view of the Severn River and the small cemetery of the Academy. Mahan is not buried there, but his spirit tramps among those gravestones, so many of them marking the final resting place of such great admirals of U.S. naval history as

Ernest King, Arleigh Burke, and James Stockdale. All of them spent more time at sea than Mahan and were vastly more distinguished in the handling of ships and sailors, but none of them can surpass Mahan in contributions—both practical and theoretical—to the profession of naval service. Nor can any of them match the impact he had on the very idea of sea power as a foundational element of the global influence of the United States. We all sail today in Mahan's considerable intellectual shadow when we contemplate the oceans and why the United States must be deeply engaged there.

One of the most prized items in that office at Annapolis is the logbook that is the original "proceedings" of the U.S. Naval Institute, including the minutes of the founding meeting of eight commissioned Navy officers in Newport, Rhode Island, in 1886. It is written in a spidery hand, but the names and signatures are clear—including that of Cdr. Alfred Thayer Mahan. He would be proud, I think, to know how the Institute has grown; today, it counts more than 50,000 members, both officer and enlisted; convenes conferences on the big defense issues of our day; publishes more than eighty titles annually; maintains a superb library with over 400,000 images, hundreds of oral histories, and thousands of books; and maintains a staff of dedicated professionals who carry on Admiral Mahan's legacy every day.

My relationship with Mahan endures to this day. Over the course of four decades, I have written for the *Proceedings* magazine at every stage of my career and authored or coauthored six books (this being the seventh) with the Naval Institute Press.[2] All of that began for me—and for many others—with Alfred Thayer Mahan. In an early fitness report, Mahan was infamously slammed with the admonition, "it is not the business of naval officers to write books." Count me grateful that he was undeterred: we are all richer for his continued writing—as a Navy, as a profession, and as a nation. But, most importantly, he brought the eye of the nation to the importance of the seas, and thus is a fundamental part of the chain that connects our nation to the oceans. He did that most specifically with the publication in 1890 of his most important book.

Mahan's defining work was *The Influence of Sea Power upon History, 1660–1783*, a book sweeping in tone, scope, and ambition.[3] Fittingly, he began the work that would become the book while on a nine-month sabbatical from the Navy. Recently tapped by Adm. Stephen B. Luce, founder of the Naval War College, to join the faculty in Newport, Rhode Island, Mahan asked for and received permission to delay his arrival until the start of the following academic year. In the interim, as described above, he went to New York (ostensibly under Luce's orders but effectively without supervision) and began researching on the topics he was contracted to teach.

Although it followed a somewhat tortuous path to publication, *The Influence of Sea Power Upon History, 1660–1783* (expanded in a second volume through 1812) eventually became an international bestseller. Interestingly, the book was initially better received in Europe (particularly in Britain and Germany) than in the United States, but what it lacked in breadth of influence, it made up for in the influence of those who understood it. Fellow naval historian and future president Theodore Roosevelt read it in a weekend and called it "a *very* good book"; indeed, as undersecretary of the Navy and especially as president, he would cement Mahan's influence by building the Great White Fleet—the first truly modern U.S. fleet. If Mahan had laid the cornerstone, Roosevelt built upon it the foundation of U.S. naval power that would go into World War I less than a decade after the Great White Fleet made its round-the-world cruise (and put the world on notice) from 1907 to 1909.

The complexity of the book and its importance to how we view the seas cannot easily be summarized in a short essay, but Mahan essentially points out how sea power enabled the rise of Great Britain and often protected it from continental foes; the need for attention and resources for national maritime fleets, both military and commercial; the criticality of protecting sea lanes of communication, the trade routes around the world ocean; providing for forward operations through a system of logistic and resupply bases; and the potential value of blockades in warfare. He walks through a number of American and European conflicts in making these points. His essential theory of sea power remains very much in vogue today, both for the established global maritime power of the United States and especially for the rising naval power that is China. If we end up in a conflict with China—God forbid—it will be fought in many ways along the lines of Mahan's theory and practice.

This is a not always an "easy" book to read—indeed, it is anything but a "page turner." But even in a show as popular as *Game of Thrones*, we find distinct echoes of Mahan in the application of sea power and the character of the sea rover Euron Greyjoy, who uses the oceans to redefine global history in his world. If a reader wants to truly understand the importance of the seas on the history of the world—and, more importantly, on the future—it is a mandatory book to reside on *The Sailor's Bookshelf*.

CHAPTER FORTY-SIX

THE NAVY AS A FIGHTING MACHINE

by Bradley A. Fiske

His inventions virtually outfitted the bridge of the American
warships that fought in [both] world wars.[1]

I have deep admiration for many, many admirals in history. I wrote a book about some of the best, stretching back 2,500 years to Themistocles, the ancient Greek who led the Athenian fleet at the pivotal battle of Salamis against the Persians.[2] In that book I introduced the reader to ten remarkable naval leaders and weighed their character and accomplishments in a series of essays, culminating with Rear Adm. Grace Hopper, the twentieth-century woman who led the Navy kicking and screaming into the computer age. One admiral who did not quite make that top ten list, but for whom I have great respect, was a turn-of-the-last century naval leader, Bradley Fiske.

What I like most about Admiral Fiske (besides the fact that he shared my vertically challenged status at a shade under five foot six inches) was his "renaissance man" qualities. He was first and foremost a consummate seaman who could drive a ship—by sail or power—with the best of his generation and commanded three major warships. Fiske was also an inventor who could roll up his sleeves and invent a new device, welding and screwing together metal and wood and creating, for example, the stadimeter—a device still used on the bridge of every ship in the Navy to tell the distance to another vessel. It was highly useful, especially in the days before radar. Fiske was also key in the invention of the engine order telegraph, a very clever way to relay orders from the bridge down to the engine room, many decks below. Over the course of a very long life (he lived to be nearly eighty-eight), Fiske invented more than 130 devices and provided immensely useful technical descriptions so others could profit from his brilliance. He was perhaps the most revolutionary naval inventor of all time.

After graduating from the Naval Academy with the class of 1875, he served on steam vessels in both the Atlantic and Pacific. Fiske was also assigned to the Bureau of Ordnance, where he began to develop a reputation as an innovator. During the late 1800s he was deeply involved in the commissioning and outfitting of USS *Atlanta*, one of the Navy's first truly modern steel warships. "Fiske's improvements were looked upon with critical misgivings by conservative-minded senior officers, but in nearly every instance his works proved successful and in the case of his telescopic gunsight, revolutionary."[3] His last major invention, in 1921, was an early version of a microfilm reader.

As he climbed the career ladder, making rear admiral in 1911, Fiske was widely regarded as one of the most technically astute and capable mariners, tacticians, and technologists in the Navy. By the start of World War I, he was the aide for operations to the secretary of the Navy, a position that evolved into today's chief of naval operations (CNO). He saw U.S. involvement in the war coming and wrote convincingly about the Navy's lack of preparation. This blunt assessment was central to his being passed over for selection as the first CNO and subsequent premature retirement. "Fiske had sacrificed his own naval future in the campaign for the [creation of the position of] Chief of Naval Operations," according to one study.[4] This occurred in 1915–16, and his writings led eventually to an outpouring of critical analysis of the Navy's state of readiness. In all of this, Fiske kept the central objective in mind that a Navy's purpose is sea control and power projection.

All of that is extremely impressive. But he lands on *The Sailor's Bookshelf* because Rear Admiral Fiske was also a persuasive and thoughtful operational maritime thinker and writer. His principal manifesto, *The Navy as a Fighting Machine*, is still read and studied by naval professionals and security analysts who seek to understand the impact of the oceans on military strategy and fleet operations. Published in 1916, it is a seaman's book, truly focused on how to employ warships most effectively globally. In this, his thinking accurately reflected his experience as a sailor in the most distant stations of the Atlantic and Pacific Oceans. As Fiske said, "If one watches a fleet of ships moving on the sea, he gets an impression of tremendous power. But if he watches Niagara [Falls], or the thunder-storm, is a power that belongs to Niagara or the thunder-storm and not to man. Man cannot control the power of Niagara or the thunder-storm; but he can control the power of a fleet."[5] As he develops this point, it is clear that he means that the fundamental relationship of navies is centered in their ability to apply power in a distributed way across great distances and at specific chokepoints on the surface of the earth.[6] He eventually wrote six books, the last of which was *Invention: The Master-Key to Progress*.

He was also a prescient strategic analyst. He served as president of the U.S. Naval Institute, the intellectual heart of the naval profession, for eleven years, 1912–23, thinking, writing, and publishing constantly. As late as 1924 he was still commenting on international affairs, correctly predicting the inevitability of a U.S.–Japanese war. He lived to see that dire proclamation come to pass with the 1941 attack on Pearl Harbor in his eighty-seventh year but sadly not quite long enough to see the pivotal battle of Midway in the early summer of 1942 turn the tide in the Pacific.[7] One hopes he was in heaven cheering on the fleet all the way to Tokyo Bay and reflecting with deserved pride on the hand his inventions and thinking had in the success of the American fleet. No one in our naval history had quite the nexus of his expertise in technology and mastery of naval operations in the context of the deep ocean battlefield. Bradley Fiske was unique and, as a maritime inventor who also commanded ships and fleets, quite unmatched.

CHAPTER FORTY-SEVEN

THE PERFECT STORM
A True Story of Men against the Sea

by Sebastian Junger

It's no fish ye're buying, it's men's lives.

— Sir Walter Scott[1]

eople ask me from time to time, "What's the worst storm you've been in at sea?" And sometimes they will even say, "Were you ever scared that your ship couldn't handle the seas and might sink?" Fortunately, the answer to the second question is simple: nope, in all my years at sea I've never felt that I was on a ship that might sink. But I've certainly been in my share of bad storms, including a hurricane off the Atlantic coast in the early 1990s and a very bad set of coastal storms in the Bass Strait, which separates Tasmania from the southern tip of Australia (really at the bottom of the world), in 1999. I was never really worried because of the size of my ships (an 8,000-ton destroyer for the first, and a 100,000-ton aircraft carrier for the second). I had also had the benefit of having studied naval architecture at Annapolis and understanding how buoyancy works—that ships can roll very dramatically but will "snap back" so long as basic principles are followed and hull integrity is preserved.

Having said that, I was always deeply aware of the dangers of exceeding the maximum roll my ships were designed to handle. As Sebastian Junger says in *The Perfect Storm*, "Every boat has a degree of roll from which she can no longer recover."[2] This is called the "righting arm" and the "righting moment," both of which he explains in some depth in this brilliant and multifaceted book. When I was headed out to major command at sea, about to be a commodore in command of a group of five destroyers, a cruiser, and a frigate, an old friend of mine gave me a copy of Junger's book. He inscribed it to "A new commodore," and wrote that "It is a good read. And a good lesson." I read the book cover to cover in a night. It is a powerful cautionary tale that every mariner should read from time to time.

The book tells the story of a potent storm that hit the coast of North America in the fall of 1991 and focuses on the sinking of a long-line swordfish boat, *Andrea Gail*. The relatively small boat was roughly six hundred miles off the coast when all contact was lost, leading to the deaths of the crew of six experienced mariners under command of Capt. Billy Tyne. Junger does a superb job bringing to life each of the sailors, providing a poignant backstory for the crew. Another aspect of the story is the tale of the rescue of the crew of the sailboat *Sartori* by a Coast Guard cutter under incredibly heroic circumstances amid the worst of the storm. All of the characters on *Andrea Gail* were fairly to extremely experienced mariners who lived near the ship's home port of Gloucester, Massachusetts.

But the real star of the book is the storm itself, created by the combination of a classic nor'easter that then absorbed Hurricane Grace, which then became a small (but intense, in a confined geographic area) hurricane itself. Occurring late in the hurricane season of 1991, the storm ultimately caused several hundred million dollars in damage ashore and created waves well over thirty feet at sea. One weather buoy recorded a wave of over one hundred feet. Junger does an outstanding job simply describing the weather effects that combined to create an unexpected and deadly system, especially so late in the year. The track of the storm looks bizarre, even to a casual observer as it came down from the northeast, pivoted off the mid-Atlantic, then spun back to New England. He starts the story: "Dawn at sea, a grey void emerging out of a vaster black one. 'The earth was without form and darkness was upon the face of the deep.' Whoever wrote that knew the sea—knew the pale emergence of the world every morning, a world that contained absolutely nothing, not one thing."[3] The calm, quite literally, before the storm. The description of the impact of the storm and its effect on *Andrea Gail* and *Satori* as well as on the larger Coast Guard cutter is powerfully rendered. As Junger says, "A mature hurricane is by far the most powerful event on earth; the combined nuclear arsenals of the U.S. and the former Soviet Union don't contain enough energy to keep a hurricane going for one day."[4] Again and again, the author brings us back to the storm and the sea.

Bonus: The 2000 film version of *The Perfect Storm* is very good. It was deservedly a big hit, including star turns by George Clooney and Diane Lane, and was nominated for Academy Awards for Best Visual Effects and Best Sound. Another tragedy at sea is recounted in Rachel Slade's 2018 book *Into the Raging Sea: Thirty-Three Mariners, One Megastorm,* and *the Sinking of* El Faro, an account of the 2015 loss of a merchant vessel in the Atlantic during Hurricane Joaquin.

CHAPTER
FORTY-EIGHT

THE SEAFARERS
Time-Life twenty-two-volume
series, 1978–81

*by various expert authors and the editorial
staff of Time-Life Books* [1]

Perhaps it seems odd to include this series of beautifully illustrated and superbly written books on this list. After all, it is not a single volume, as are all the other selections on *The Sailor's Bookshelf*. But just as a ship needs an anchor, a sailor's bookshelf needs a fundamental set of books to lay out the entirety of mankind's relationship to the sea. This is that series, and it could not be better done. I collected my set over about twenty years, picking up one or two in used bookstores. I ended up with a handful of duplicates, which I've given away individually as gifts when I thought the subject would be of particular interest to a friend—say the volume on pirates to a couple headed to the Caribbean for a vacation. In addition to *The Seafarers*, the Time-Life team created a large number of other sets (around seventy) on themes like photography, foods of the world, the "Old West," American Indians, the Civil War, the history of the world, the American wilderness, and many, many other subjects. The books in each series were mailed on a monthly basis to households that had signed up to receive them, essentially as part of a book club, and the series were quite popular in the mid- to late twentieth century. I've dipped in and out of the many of the other offerings in the Time-Life library but, to my mind, none match *The Seafarers* for completeness and pure beauty. But then I might be biased.

Every volume is handsomely bound, oversized, and printed on archival paper. They are lavishly illustrated and run just under two hundred pages each, and a highlight is that each includes a two-page spread that has a cut-out view of a specific ship—a frigate from the age of fighting sail, a luxury liner, a Viking longboat, and so on. The twenty-two volumes are all highly readable and written by a team of expert authors, closely edited by the Time-Life team. As a writer myself for *Time*—I do a monthly column for them—I know firsthand how detail-oriented (the word persnickety comes to mind) the Time-Life editors are. Sadly, *Life* magazine has departed for the great editorial desk in the sky, but the DNA of that highly visual publication has clearly seeped into the truly extraordinary selection of maps, charts, paintings, photographs, and various visual representations of the seafarer's story. Each book has a thickly padded, black leatherette cover with design and lines embossed on spine and covers. There is gold-colored printing on the spine and front covers, and each cover has an evocative print pasted on it. The printing dates and authors vary, but the writers are expert in every regard.

While the books were gradually published and released in the late 1970s and early 1980s, there is a 1990 reprint of the entire set that is widely available through the used-book market, including on Amazon or AbeBooks sites. Typically, the set can be had for well under $10 per volume for books in reasonably used condition, which is truly superb value for the money. Individual volumes in the set run around $5 to $10, so they can be gradually collected for even less money. And for someone who simply wants the entire set in essentially new condition, there are such offers online in the range of $350 or so, still a fantastic buy at around $15 per book. While the history coverage ends in the mid-1980s, given the sweep of the voyage, this is still a quite exceptional representation of how men and women have gone down to the sea in ships over the millennia.

Herewith the volumes:

Each of the volumes originally came with a separate "editor's note" that explained the basics of the book, and most of them included a detached map or chart. In the used editions, these have often passed into the mists of time, but if buying a volume, finding one with those detached documents is a plus.

Whether you choose to buy them as an online package or find them one at a time over a yearslong search, these are volumes that truly reward the reader. My personal favorites are *The Windjammers* and *The Racing Yachts*, probably because I did not have a strong sense of either of those two cultures. But every book in this series is a treasure—which can be a stand-alone entry on *The Sailor's Bookshelf* by itself, but as part of a larger library you will find yourself going back to each again and again to connect with other volumes.

Bonus: Another Time-Life book series is *World War II*, which is thirty-nine volumes. The seagoing Navy volumes in that series are quite exceptional, including *The Battle of the Atlantic, War in the Pacific,* and *The Mediterranean.* This series offers the same quality but examines nautical history from a slightly different perspective than *The Seafarers.*

CHAPTER FORTY-NINE

TRAILBLAZER
The U.S. Navy's First Black Admiral

by Vice Adm. Samuel L. Gravely Jr., USN, with Paul Stillwell

My life changed in January of 1960 when I received
orders to destroyer duty.[1]

I met Adm. Sam Gravely just before the turn of the century at an event organized by the U.S. Naval Institute. He had always been someone for whom I had deep respect given his impressive string of "firsts": first Black officer on a U.S. Navy warship, first Black Navy commander, first Black warship commanding officer, first Black captain, first Black rear admiral, and of course first Black vice admiral. We met and chatted at the behest of Paul Stillwell, an extraordinary naval historian who has conducted many, many vital oral histories of famous naval officers. These are essentially a series of taped interviews in which the interviewer gently guides the long-retired admiral through a verbal voyage covering the years of his or her life and career. Paul Stillwell is an acknowledged master at this delicate art. I have done one myself, and it is an interesting and introspective experience, and Paul made it a good one.

After he introduced me to Admiral Gravely—a relaxed but large and imposing man—I told the admiral that we were nearly shipmates. What I meant was
that just a few years after he relinquished command of a guided missile cruiser,
USS *Jouett* (CG 29), in 1971, I had sailed on the ship as a midshipman. As I
told him, I went to sea for the first time in "his cruiser" (although at the time
it was designated a guided missile frigate or "destroyer leader," to be precise).
He enjoyed hearing that, and for a few moments I was wrapped into the warm
memories of this exceptional pioneer of naval service. He was selected for promotion to rear admiral while in command of *Jouett*, and it clearly had a very
warm place in his heart. As he writes in *Trailblazer*, "*Jouett* was a beautiful ship
and a good deal larger than a destroyer of those days. It was 547 feet long and
displaced almost eight thousand tons. Because it was a major command, the
ship was blessed with a great deal of talent, both enlisted men and officers."[2]
After my discussion with him, I went away thinking the Navy was lucky to have
such a man sail first in the formation of Black officers to sea. He passed away a
few years later, in 2004, but he still looms large in my memory—especially during these troubled times in America as we grapple with our imperfect history
of race relations.

Trailblazer is compiled from the tapes of the interviews with Vice Admiral
Gravely conducted by Paul Stillwell, so the reader is treated to the voice of
"Sammie the Sailor" (as his wife called him) on every page of this short but
very impactful book. And that voice, perhaps softened a bit by the years, is very
compelling: friendly, even-handed, full of humor and common sense in equal
measure, humble, and suffused with a quiet determination to succeed despite
all the obvious obstacles placed ahead of him. Above all, to me, there is a love
of the ocean and the sea and the art of shiphandling and the leading of sailors
that shines through everything and ties the book together. As he said about his
tour as executive officer (second in command) in USS *Theodore E. Chandler*, a
destroyer, "Whenever we were operating with a carrier—in a storm or in any
kind of intense operations—the skipper was generally on the bridge. I would go
up to the bridge for most evolutions and certainly I'd be up on the bridge when
the captain felt it was a ticklish situation. I was on the bridge just about all the
time he was there, and sometimes I took over when he needed some rest."[3] That
is the kind of executive officer to have, believe me.

Born in Richmond, Virginia, Gravely relates the story of heading off to the Navy in 1942 (after the Army rejected him for a supposed heart murmur). Gravely was commissioned just a few months after the "Golden Thirteen" (the very first Black officers in the U.S. Navy). He went immediately to sea and stayed there for the bulk of his long career, including service in a submarine chaser, the battleship *Iowa*, and the *Chandler*, as mentioned above. His first of several commands at sea was the destroyer escort USS *Falgout* followed by the destroyer USS *Taussig*. He saw a good deal of combat operations off the coast of Vietnam during the war and began to develop a real specialization in communications.

After making captain, he was ordered to the new guided missile frigate (later a cruiser) USS *Jouett*, where he had a particularly successful command tour. I remember being pleasantly surprised during my two-month-long midshipman cruise on board *Jouett* being invited to dine (once) with the commanding officer. As I entered the relatively impressive cabin, I was doubly pleasantly surprised to see the face of the previous commanding officer framed outside the door—a Black face. I didn't appreciate at the time just how hard that trail must have been for Gravely to blaze.

That tour in *Jouett* led to his selection to flag rank and becoming director of naval communications as a rear admiral. The pinnacle of his career was command of the Navy's storied Third Fleet, based in San Diego, California. As he said with relish of his command of the fleet, at the time the largest in the United States, "From the time a ship began its workups for deployment, it was under my operational command. The ship belonged to me, and the skipper took his orders from me until he moved under the control of Commander Seventh Fleet at an appropriate time when he was going west. I had absolute control until then."[4]

Gravely had a wonderful marriage with his wife, Alma. They had three children, although one died tragically in a car accident while the admiral was stationed at Pearl Harbor. Every page of his book reflects the stability and warmth of his relationship with Alma, who was his "anchor to windward." When the Navy appropriately named a beautiful *Arleigh Burke*–class destroyer after him, USS *Gravely*, she christened the ship. He would have been beaming down from heaven in 2010 when that happened. In *Trailblazer*, Alma almost steals the show from the admiral with her "afterword," which is a short but beautifully realized set of reminiscences about life as a Navy wife. One anecdote is so accurate and reflective of all that Navy spouses give: "After our arrival in a new place, even when our heads were down in boxes and we hadn't found the curtains or the sheets yet, he used to say: 'When are we going to have the first party?' I would say, 'Can't you just let me find the curtains?'"[5]

The admiral lived to be eighty-two years old, and as Alma said after both a Navy destroyer and an elementary school were named for him, "It is truly fitting that both a warship and a school are named for him, because they embody the values he cherished throughout his life."[6]

Your navy remembers you well, Admiral, your love of your family, your sailors, and your life at sea. Sail proud, sir.

Bonus: *The Golden Thirteen: Recollections of the First Black Naval Officers*, a collection of oral histories also edited by Paul Stillwell, tells the stories of the first thirteen Black men to become commissioned naval officers. Theirs are proud stories as well, but none blazed the trail that Vice Admiral Gravely did. Their stories are a nice complement to this singular memoir.

CHAPTER FIFTY

TWO YEARS BEFORE THE MAST
A Personal Narrative of Life at Sea

by Richard Henry Dana Jr.

There is a witchery in the sea, its songs and stories, and in the mere sight of a ship, and the sailor's dress, especially to a young mind, which has done more to man navies, and fill merchantmen, than all the pressgangs of Europe.[1]

T his is a workmanlike book—a sailor's journal in essence, appearing in 1840 and remaining in print until the present day—about a young man's two-year voyage from Boston to California and back. It was recommended to me by my sixth-grade geography teacher when I lived with my parents in Southern California. Mrs. Dodge said it was a sea story, a coming-of-age tale, and a portrait of early California. The first two are pretty obvious even to an early teenager, but I was surprised to learn of the unflattering depiction of the "Golden State" embedded in the book, which is far from complimentary. Indeed, Dana at one point in the book says, "The Californians are an idle, thriftless people, and can make nothing for themselves."² How times have changed. The state is now the fifth-largest economy in the world. While the description of the time Dana spends ashore is interesting, the real power in this nineteenth-century account—written by a contemporary of Herman Melville—is in its clear, honest, and, to my mind, gorgeous descriptions of the oceans.

And yes it is a coming-of-age story, to be sure. Early in the book, we learn that Dana, a well-educated upper-class lad, is determined to go to sea to improve his eyesight and constitution. He had suffered an attack of measles while student at Harvard, which had damaged his eyesight. He chose the life of a common sailor (hence the title, as the junior sailors slung their hammocks before the mast and below decks) and kept a journal throughout the voyage. But as he discovers quickly, "there is not so helpless and pitiable an object in the world as a landsman beginning a sailor's life."³ On the outbound leg in the brig *Pilgrim*, he begins to get his sea legs and literally "learn the ropes." The ship's mission was trading cargo from the United States to what was then the Mexican colony of California. The ship conducted business along the string of settlements in mid-nineteenth-century California, including San Diego, San Pedro, Santa Barbara, Monterey, and San Francisco. As I reread the book now, I look at the description of San Pedro with particular interest, having served as second in command of a cruiser based in that location, now the port of Los Angeles, in the late 1980s. Dana presciently remarks that eventually that great bay of San Francisco will be the heart of California's commerce with the world.

The portrait of early California that emerges is fascinating, but the real heart of the book unfolds on his voyage home. As he embarks for the return on another ship, the similarly sized *Alert*, he is much more confident in his nautical skills and observations. The best sections of the book are the descriptions of the voyage around Cape Horn at the tip of South America. His prose alternates between appreciation of the incredible natural beauty and the sheer terror of monstrous seas and icebergs. As a sailor, he faced huge winds and waves as he climbed up and down the masts to rig the sails. I have rounded the Horn several times, most recently in a U.S. Navy nuclear-powered aircraft carrier of some 100,000 tons. Even in a vast city-ship like USS *Abraham Lincoln*, I worried about the wind and seas; Dana is a better sailor than I to have rounded in such a relatively tiny sailing vessel. There are injuries, scurvy, and floggings described in detail in his memoir, but it is the sea that is both the beauty and the beast in this tale.

After rounding the Horn and heading for home, there are quiet moments of reflection: "So quiet, too, was the sea, and so steady the breeze, that if these sails had been sculptured marble they could not have been more motionless. Not a ripple upon the surface of the canvas; not even a quivering of the extreme edges of the sail, so perfectly were they distended by the breeze."[4] At this stage of his maturation, Dana sees and objects to the oppressive life of a junior sailor at sea. Indeed, there is a real political agenda in the book that was much in keeping with Dana's later life. Ironically, the book became notable as a sort of informal guide to life in California after the gold rush increased vastly the interest.

Later in life Dana became a determined and well-known champion of the underdog, from working for the freedom of African American slaves in the South to helping seaman who were "pressed" into service. He attended Harvard Law School (at the time the Dane Law School) and specialized in admiralty law. Among his many books is *The Seaman's Friend: A Treatise on Practical Seamanship*, a sort of coda on the legal privileges of merchant sailors. In addition to his sailing memoir of *Two Years before the Mast*, he edited and wrote various legal works. In the run-up to the American Civil War, he was highly active in defending slaves and freedmen in the Northern courts and eventually became the U.S. attorney for the commonwealth of Massachusetts, appointed by Abraham Lincoln.

I've loved this book since I was a very young teenager, and it played no small role in my eventual conversion to sailor. And I often recommend it to friends as an introduction to the sea, a window into a young man's journey to maturity, an early treatise on civil rights, and, yes, a portrait of California before it became the crowded megastate it is today. The book succeeds in all those veins, but above all the reader will be moved by the power and the glory of the wind and waves.

Bonus: Obviously, the book connects with Melville and his entire oeuvre, but it is also a nice fit alongside the works of Patrick O'Brian.

CONCLUSION

A nd so we come to the end of our voyage together. The fifty books here are but a tiny fraction of the hundreds of thousands of books published over the years about the world's oceans. I could as easily have selected one hundred, or two hundred, or five hundred books to "know the sea"—and still only scratched the surface. But these will do as at least an initial set of sea buoys, a sort of channel out to the deeper ocean where so many more good volumes can be found. *The Sailor's Bookshelf* is too small. Suitable books could easily fill a "Sailor's Library."

In that spirit, let me offer three thoughts.

The first is simple: keep reading about the oceans. So much of the voyage of the human race on this planet will ultimately depend on our knowledge and appreciation about the vast world ocean—as a resource for protein, carbohydrates, water, energy, and oxygen; as a global commons across which the world's trade will flow if we are smart enough to avoid turning it into the battlefield it so often has been in history; and an inspiration for art and literature, as I hope some of these books have offered. And as the oceans enter a particularly dangerous phase in their life, as the planet warms and we pollute them, we need people who appreciate the sea in all its magnificence and splendor. Read and you will become an advocate for the oceans in every way. In that sense, read as though the planet's life depends on it—because it will.

My second thought is that, as a sea reader, you have an obligation to find new and perhaps better books than these for your own reading list and the recommendations you provide others. Some readers will want to dive much deeper into the world of exploration; others will be intrigued to learn more about the science and environmental issues; still others will want to learn more about navigation and shiphandling and ocean racing. Your mission is to find the books that most perfectly match up with your own deepest sense of the sea. In that regard, of sailing through the thicket of books, I've asked a fellow naval officer and sea captain, Cdr. J. D. Kristenson, to craft a sort of guide path to reading the fifty books here and to offer a few thoughts of his own. You will find his suggestions in the afterword, "A Course to Steer By." May he serve as a fellow sea reader to all who have sailed this far through *The Sailor's Bookshelf.*

Finally, I'd like to leave you with fifteen additional books and an epic poem that *almost* made this "nifty fifty." Perhaps one of these would fit with your own reading program better than one or two of the ones I've chosen—so be it. In a sense, approaching a book is a bit like approaching an island in the deep ocean: it can be described to you, but until you arrive off the coast, come ashore, and walk the ground, you never really know it. So here are a final set of distant islands to consider as you move on from *The Sailor's Bookshelf* on the voyage of sea reading:

1. *Asia's Cauldron: The South China Sea and the End of a Stable Pacific,* by Robert Kaplan—Kaplan guides the reader on a walk around the difficult waters of the South China Sea, which—God forbid—could become the scene of a conflict between the United States and China, dragging in the many nations that surround it. Think of it as a cautionary tale of sorts.[1]

2. *Great Naval Battles of the Twentieth Century,* by Jean-Yves Delitte and Giuseppe Baiguera—This graphic text is an easy and enjoyable way to look at some of the most important and pivotal battles in human history, many of which are described in E. B. Potter's superb book, *Sea Power: A Naval History.*[2]

3. *Sea Power: The History and Geopolitics of the World's Ocean,* by James Stavridis (hmm, name sounds familiar)—In this book, the "characters" are not people but rather the oceans and seas of the world. For each, I try to tell the story of the geography, economy, history, and current place in the geopolitical landscape of this turbulent twenty-first century. It essentially picks up where E. B. Potter leaves off in his earlier work.[3]

4. *The Sea Plays of Eugene O'Neill*—One of the great American playwrights, this winner of the Nobel Prize in Literature wrote a collection of one-act plays that capture the merchant sailor's lonely existence. They are normally packaged as a single volume of seven plays, four of which are loosely connected. Sad, moving, at times funny, the plays are the work of a master writer.[4]

5. *A Thread across the Ocean: The Heroic Story of the Transatlantic Cable*, by John Steele Gordon—This story of the first communications cable is a triumph of science and determination over the most difficult maritime conditions in the mid-1800s.[5]

6. *Into the Kingdom of Ice: The Grand and Terrible Polar Voyage of the USS Jeannette*, by Hampton Sides—Written by a master historian, this is a dark tale of an expedition gone terribly wrong, the "grand and terrible" polar voyage of the USS *Jeannette* in the late 1800s.[6]

7. *Over the Edge of the World*, by Laurence Bergreen—This is the best single biography of Ferdinand Magellan, the first man to lead an expedition that circumnavigated the earth.[7]

8. *The Admirals: Nimitz, Halsey, Leahy, and King—The Five-Star Admirals Who Won the War at Sea*, by Walter Borneman—Four of the most important American naval commanders of the twentieth century, and how their lives and careers were intertwined, are at the heart of this fine book: Nimitz, Halsey, Leahy, and King.[8]

9. *Decision at Sea: Five Naval Battles that Shaped American History*, by Craig Symonds—Covered in this book are the five most important sea battles in American history: Lake Erie in the War of 1812; the Civil War battle between ironclads *Monitor* and *Merrimack*; Dewey's triumph at the Battle of Manila Bay in the Spanish-American War; the triumph (by a whisker) at Midway in World War II; and the Arabian Gulf battle between the United States and Iran, Operation Praying Mantis.[9]

10. *The North Water*, by Ian McGuire—This is a brutal, graphic, difficult-to-read novel about murder and rape on a whaling ship in the mid-nineteenth century. Think Cormac McCarthy (*Blood Meridian* and *All the Pretty Horses*) goes to sea. It is a challenging book in which good and evil battle on the landscape of the sea.[10]

11. *Billy Budd, Sailor*, by Herman Melville—This is not on the list simply because of the obvious and necessary inclusion of Melville's masterpiece, *Moby-Dick*. But *Billy Budd* is a superb, tragic, and meaningful novella about a handsome and popular young sailor falsely accused of instigating mutiny in the British navy in the late 1700s. The captain feels compelled to administer the harshest of punishments, despite fundamentally believing in the goodness of the "angel," Billy. Ultimately a novel about the conflict between law and justice in the difficult crucible of a warship, it resonates to this day.[11]

12. *Delilah: A Novel*, by Marcus Goodrich—This powerful 1941 novel describes life on an American destroyer, *Delilah*, serving in the Pacific during World War I. It is notable as a realistic description of life "below decks" for enlisted sailors. *Delilah* remained the biggest success for writer Goodrich, who is perhaps better known today as the first husband of actress Olivia de Havilland.[12]

13. *The Two-Ocean War: A Short History of the United States Navy in the Second World War*, by Samuel Eliot Morison—The author, a historian who served as a naval officer himself, wrote a highly regarded definitive study of U.S. naval operations in World War II in a fifteen-volume series. This work synthesizes and compresses the series into a single readable volume.[13]

14. *The Last Stand of the Tin Can Sailors*, by James Hornfischer—This gripping account is told from the deckplates of the heroic charge of a group of destroyer escorts against massive Japanese battleships and cruisers at the height of the Battle of Leyte Gulf. Their efforts probably saved tens of thousands of American lives in the lightly defended landing force.[14]

15. *Trade and Dominion: The European Oversea Empires in the Eighteenth Century*, by J. H. Parry—This vibrant history details the ways in which the oceans became the route by which European powers (United Kingdom, France, Spain, the Netherlands, and Portugal, principally) built massive overseas empires following the age of discovery. This extremely well-researched volume leads with a deep focus on the nautical aspects of the colonization of much of the world.[15]

16. *Rime of the Ancient Mariner*, by Samuel Taylor Coleridge—This is not a book, of course, but a long epic poem written in the late 1700s. It is a tale full of magical realism and memorable images by a renowned British poet. As an "ancient mariner" myself, it seems a good place to stop.[16]

No doubt many readers will finish *The Sailor's Bookshelf* and say to themselves: "I can't believe he left off my favorite book!" If you find yourself in that category, go to my website, AdmiralStav.com, and find the contact page, https://admiralstav.com/contact/. Drop me a line with your suggestion and perhaps someday it will make it into a second edition of this mission.

It has been a pleasure sailing alongside you for this voyage. Godspeed and open water in all your future voyages on the endless sea of ocean literature.

AFTERWORD

A COURSE TO STEER BY

by Cdr. J. D. Kristenson, USN

If you want to build a ship, don't drum up people to collect
wood and don't assign them tasks and work, but rather
teach them to long for the endless immensity of the sea.

—Antoine de Saint-Exupéry

his book grew out of twin loves, a love of the sea and a love of books;
it simply could not have been be written by someone whose life was not
awash with both. Ancient mariners set their course and crossed oceans
guided only by the stars. Over the last four decades of his distinguished career,
Admiral Stavridis has accomplished an equally impressive feat of intellectual
navigation, assembling a constellation of great literature that has illuminated his
path from one waypoint to another.

It is important to reemphasize that the selection presented here is part of a much
larger canon and is not meant to be comprehensive or even prescriptive. Books can
only be placed in direct context with the books that precede and follow them. In
another way, books stand outside of time entirely and are in constant dialogue with
one another, and this book is no exception. These fifty "aids to navigation" provide a

solution to a problem every reader eventually encounters: a seemingly infinite number of books set against a very finite amount of time available to read.

In the *Book of the Way*, Lao Tzu wrote "when the student is ready, the teacher will appear." It is much the same with great books that speak to our own experience. Not every book will serve every reader at each stage of their reading journey. Some books may be picked up and set down again if the time is not right. Some will spill forth all of their lessons in a single reading, while others will only reveal their wisdom in waves after many readings. United only by the sea, the books recommended here are wildly divergent in topic and style. As a result, there are a great number of ways to move through this book. With that in mind, I would like to suggest a three-tiered approach to this book, inspired by the rank structure of the Merchant Marines: Able Seaman, Mate, and Master.

The Able Seaman's List

Perhaps you do not own a boat but relish any opportunity to spend time on the water. If you do have a boat of your own, maybe it is in a freshwater lake. This is enjoyable, and yet you still feel the pull of the larger ocean. Those with a general or budding interest in the seas will profit most from a sampling of one book from each of the four categories. I recommend that you start with the following, in order:

Moby-Dick
Longitude
The Endurance
The Perfect Storm

Melville's classic, *Moby-Dick*, can credibly lay claim to not only being the greatest sea novel, but the Great American Novel. *Longitude* will provide the reader context of the amazing technical challenges early sailors faced anytime they left sight of land. *The Endurance* and *The Perfect Storm* stand in stark contrast to one another and examine the will of man to overcome the death grip of the sea and when that grip becomes too brutal to resist. Each of these books dovetails nicely with the next, and reading them together will give readers who are still relatively unacquainted with the sea a sense of the many ways in which it is a truly unforgiving domain.

The Mate's List

Perhaps you are a recreational sailor or grew up in a coastal town. Born with salt water in your veins, the sea has been a part of your life for as long as you can remember. Still, like many of us, you long to know it better. A chief enticement of books is that they are filled with the power to make us think things we like to think. The unseen danger is that we remain ignorant of many significant dimensions of the sea that lie outside our experiences. The books in part 1, "The Oceans," are particularly useful to help alleviate lingering "sea blindness." For those who see themselves among this group of readers, I recommend the following reading plan:

Atlas of Remote Islands
The Hungry Ocean
The Outlaw Ocean
The Sea around Us
The World Is Blue
The Silent World
Life of Pi
She Captains
Trailblazer

Atlas of Remote Islands will acquaint you with the far reaches of the ocean while each of the next four books (*The Hungry Ocean, The Outlaw Ocean, The Sea around Us, The World Is Blue*) will expand your horizons by shining a light on vital ocean-related topics (fishing, piracy, conservation, and the future of our oceans, respectively).

Reading well is a difficult pleasure. Books are fine companions on boring journeys, but the best also serve to move the reader forward in some way. Reading is among the very best ways to learn, but only if we intentionally seek to encounter "otherness" in our choice of what to read. Largely due to historical forces, much of what has been passed down to us in the sea literature canon is largely books written by white, male, and Western authors. However, books like *Life of Pi, She Captains,* and *Trailblazer* provide a proxy for the lived experiences of women, minorities, and other cultures and their views of the sea. Exposing oneself to these diverse and valuable perspectives is dipping one's toe into a new sea for the very first time.

The Master's List

Perhaps you are a marine biologist, work on the research vessels alongside Bob Ballard, or are a grizzled fisherman whose beard could rival a character on *Deadliest Catch*. Even if your knowledge of the sea is expansive and born of years of experience, the nature of the sea is such that it always allows us to dive a little deeper or sail a bit farther from shore. This book will be instrumental in helping you round out your understanding of the sea. Even if you generally eschew books about the military, you may be surprised by how gripping you find *Master and Commander*. If you favor more contemporary books, see what you can learn from *The Battle of Salamis* 2,500 years ago. Chances are that the books you are avoiding are the very ones that have the most to teach you.

That being said, I offer a word of caution against setting out to read all of the books as a challenge. There is a real danger of getting bogged down in a book that simply does not interest you and abandoning the effort entirely. Worse still, a reading list that is too ambitious can cause you to fall out of the habit of reading all together. For the moment, the world remains in the clutches of the COVID-19 pandemic, and it is more important than ever to select books carefully. Let your reading be like a good marriage: a natural attraction that also requires careful attention to last a lifetime. Imaginative literature from diverse perspectives connects us to otherness and, in doing so, alleviates loneliness. I urge you to find what truly speaks to you, that which can be used to help you weigh, consider, and challenge your thoughts. Grappling with a text teaches us a great deal about our own capabilities and our values. Read deeply, not to accept, not to contradict, but to grow.

As for me, I also seek to know the sea better. I am where Admiral Stavridis was before USS *Barry*, standing on the pier, once again contemplating embarking on the solemn responsibility of leading sailors at sea. I am fortunate to have the works of O'Brian, Wouk, Conrad, Melville, Hemmingway, Forster, and—after ten books oriented around the ocean—now Stavridis, with me on the journey.

Some books do not fit neatly into a certain category, and maybe this book will be the one to "sail closest to the wind" of any other on a sailor's bookshelf after all. Just as Heraclitus noted that one cannot step into the same river twice, this book makes clear the fact that one cannot sail to the same destination the same way twice; the waters are ever changing. May you return to this book over time as part of the fair winds and following seas that carry you on your voyage.

Cdr. J. D. Kristenson, USN, is a Navy surface warfare officer and an Olmsted Scholar (China). He previously commanded USS *Champion* (MCM 4), where he led a "damn fine crew of iron men on a wooden ship." He most recently served ashore as a special assistant to the supreme allied commander of NATO and is headed back to sea to lead the fight on USS *Michael Murphy* (DDG 112).

ACKNOWLEDGMENTS

S o many people have shaped my appreciation of the literature of the sea in particular, and the power of books in general, over the many years I have been reading. Let me acknowledge a few of them, regretting that inevitably I will miss so many in the need to be brief.

Let me begin with my parents, both readers throughout their lives, especially my mother. As a U.S. Marine Corps officer, my father certainly appreciated stories of the sea and was keenly aware of the long-intertwined history of the Navy and Marine Corps. Some of his earliest gifts to me were books about both services and their long history on the world's oceans. My mother, who has read more than anyone I know over her very long life—she is very healthy and reading voraciously at age ninety as I write this—has also been a giver of wonderful books over the course of my life and often suggests topics to me to this day.

At the U.S. Naval Academy, I majored in English (although, like all midshipmen in those days, I was really required to focus on science, mathematics, technology, seamanship, and engineering and graduated with a bachelor of science). Fortunately, I took a course in my major titled Literature of the Sea, which opened my eyes considerably. Throughout my four years at Annapolis, I was lucky to be exposed to a cadre of truly outstanding English professors, including most notably the department chair, Mike Jasperson, and professors Phil Jason, Fred Fetrow, and Wilson Heflin (who created the Literature of the Sea course). Over in the history department, I actually loved the Sea Power course (not all my classmates did) and took a semester from the grandmaster himself, Professor E. B. "Ned"

Potter (who had a national reputation as a Melville scholar) and a second semester with then-lieutenant Lee Martiny. To all of these teachers I owe a deep debt. Throughout my life in the Navy, I've been lucky to come in contact with many fellow enthusiasts of reading and sea literature—many of them mentors, some of them peers and shipmates at my various commands. One who truly stands out is Adm. Harry Harris, former commander of U.S. Pacific Command and the ambassador to South Korea 2018–21. His collection of modern first editions is a cause of serious "book envy" on my part, and we've been trading book recommendations for decades. Gen. Jim Mattis is a fellow serious reader and someone who always has a good book idea at the ready. Likewise, former national security advisor, retired Army lieutenant general H. R. McMaster. Others naval officers include Adm. Bob Natter, former CNO Adm. Jay Johnson, former chairman of the Joint Chiefs Adm. Mike Mullen, Gen. Sir John McCall and Gen. Richard Sherriff (my deputies at NATO), Vice Adm. Nan Direnzi and Vice Adm. Jim Houck (two of the best Navy JAGs), British Rear Adm. Ian Moncrief, Rear Adm. Bob Girrier, Rear Adm. Mark Montgomery, and Cdr. J. D. Kristenson (who has also contributed a fine afterword to this book).

On the civilian side, several of my wonderful faculty at The Fletcher School of Law and Diplomacy of Tufts University have given me dozens of ideas (especially professors John Burgess, Steve Block, Ian Johnstone, Kelly Sims Gallagher, and Bhaskar Chakravorti). Most recently, I trade book ideas with several colleagues at The Carlyle Group (David Rubenstein, Kewsong Lee, Bill Conway, Dan Daniello, and Julius Genachowski). My friends Larry Di Rita of Bank of America; Mel Immergut and his wife, Barbara; and former deputy secretary of the treasury Justin Muzinich have suggested many good books. Former ambassador Reuben Brigety has helped me often with reading thoughts as well. Former undersecretary for policy Michele Flournoy and former ambassador to the United Nations Susan Rice have given me fine book ideas as well, especially on international maritime security. The German ambassador to the United States, Emily Haber, is a reader of remarkable range as well.

As always, this book is a collaborative effort, and the team at the U.S. Naval Institute, true professionals all, have been outstanding as always. This is my seventh book with the Naval Institute Press, and it won't be my last. Vice Adm. Pete

Daly, among the best pure leaders I have met in the course of my career, continues to shape the Institute as the leading center of maritime affairs (including publishing) in this nation. He will go down in history as the best leader of the Institute since the founding days of Alfred Thayer Mahan in the late nineteenth century. My good friend and editor for this particular volume, Lt. Cdr. Tom Cutler (himself a fine sea writer), has been a joy to sail alongside once again and suggested several of the books herein.

Capt. Bill Harlow has been the best of friends, editors, and advisors since he hired me as a young commander to be speechwriter and special assistant to the secretary of the Navy, the Honorable Sean O'Keefe, nearly thirty years ago. His imprint on this book is immeasurable, as it has been on many of my other efforts, and he has my deepest thanks. No one can cut out the poetry better.

Above all, my thanks to my daughters, Christina and Julia, and my lovely wife, Laura, for putting up with all the times I seemed to sail away into an open book. For the record, no voyage in the sea of literature, no matter how absorbing or compelling, could ever compete with spending a single moment alongside the three of you.

As always, all errors of fact or opinion are mine and mine alone.

NOTES

Chapter 1. *Atlantic: Great Sea Battles, Heroic Discoveries, Titanic Storms, and a Vast Ocean of a Million Stories*

1. Simon Winchester, *Atlantic: Great Sea Battles, Heroic Discoveries, Titanic Storms, and a Vast Ocean of a Million Stories* (New York: Harper Collins, 2010), 48.

Chapter 2. *Atlas of Remote Islands: Fifty Islands I Have Never Set Foot On and Never Will*

1. Judith Schalansky, *Atlas of Remote Islands: Fifty Islands I Have Never Set Foot On and Never Will* (London: Particular, 2010), 6.
2. Schalansky, 23.
3. Robert Putman, *Early Sea Charts* (New York: Abbeville, 1983).

Chapter 3. *Cod: A Biography of the Fish that Changed the World*

1. Quoted in Mark Kurlanksy, *Cod: A Biography of the Fish that Changed the World* (New York: Walker, 1997), 29.
2. Kurlansky, 14.

Chapter 4. *Deep: Freediving, Renegade Science, and What the Ocean Tells Us about Ourselves*

1. James Nestor, *Deep: Freediving, Renegade Science, and What the Ocean Tells Us about Ourselves* (Boston: Houghton Mifflin Harcourt, 2014), 4.
2. Nestor, 6.
3. Nestor, 6.

Chapter 5. *Longitude: The True Story of a Lone Genius Who Solved the Greatest Scientific Problem of His Time*

1. Neil Armstrong, Foreword to *Longitude: The True Story of a Lone Genius Who Solved the Greatest Scientific Problem of His Time*, by Dava Sobel, 10th anniversary ed. (New York, Bloomsbury, 2005), x.

Chapter 6. *Dutton's Nautical Navigation*, 15th edition
1. Thomas J. Cutler, *Dutton's Nautical Navigation*, 15th ed. (Annapolis, Md.: Naval Institute Press, 2004), 1.

Chapter 7. *Naval Shiphandler's Guide*
1. James A. Barber, *Naval Shiphandler's Guide* (Annapolis, Md.: Naval Institute Press, 2005), 1.
2. James Stavridis, "Handling a Spruance Class Destroyer," U.S. Naval Institute *Proceedings* 105, no. 10 (October 1979): 124–26; James Stavridis, "Handling a Ticonderoga," U.S. Naval Institute *Proceedings* 113, no. 1 (January 1987): 107–9; and James Stavridis, "Handling the Arleigh Burkes," U.S. Naval Institute *Proceedings* 120, no. 10 (October 1994): 66–68.

Chapter 8. *Sea Power: A Naval History*
1. Chester Nimitz, Foreword to *Sea Power: A Naval History*, ed. by Chester Nimitz and E. B. Potter (Englewood Cliffs, N.J.: Prentice-Hall, 1960), v.
2. E. B. Potter, Preface to *Sea Power*, adapted from p. vii.

Chapter 9. *The Hungry Ocean: A Swordboat Captain's Journey*
1. Linda Greenlaw, *The Hungry Ocean: A Swordboat Captain's Journey* (New York: Hyperion, 1999), 258.
2. Greenlaw, 106.
3. Greenlaw, 234.
4. Greenlaw, 58.
5. Greenlaw, 35.
6. Greenlaw, 145.
7. *The Perfect Storm* and *The Outlaw Ocean* are covered in this book. Conrad's "The Secret Sharer" was first published in two parts in *Harper's Magazine*, August and September 1910. There are many modern publications.

Chapter 10. *The Outlaw Ocean: Journeys across the Last Untamed Frontier*
1. Ian Urbina, *The Outlaw Ocean: Journeys across the Last Untamed Frontier* (New York: Borzoi, 2019), xi.
2. Urbina, 315.
3. Urbina, xi.

Chapter 11. *The Sea around Us*
1. Rachel Carson, *The Sea around Us* (New York: Oxford University Press, 1951), 9.
2. Carson, biographic sketch on back cover.
3. Carson, 37.

4. Mathew Arnold, *The Forsaken Merman* (London: Routledge, 1854).
5. Carson, *The Sea around Us*, 173.
6. Carson, 187.
7. Carson, 216.

Chapter 12. *The World Is Blue: How Our Fate and the Ocean's Are One*
1. William McKibben, Foreword to *The World Is Blue: How Our Fate and the Ocean's Are One*, by Sylvia A. Earle (Washington, D.C.: National Geographic, 2009), 6.

Chapter 13. *Watch Officer's Guide*, 16th edition
1. Adm. James Stavridis, Rear Adm. Robert Girrier, Capt. Tom Ogden, and Capt. Jeff Heames, *Watch Officer's Guide*, 16th ed. (Annapolis, Md.: Naval Institute Press, 2020), ix.

Chapter 14. *Across the Top of the World: The Quest for the Northwest Passage*
1. Quoted in James Delgado, *Across the Top of the World* (New York: Checkmark, 1999), 171.
2. Website of Dr. James P. Delgado, https://jamesdelgado.com/books/.
3. Delgado, *Across the Top of the World*, 35–37.
4. James Stavridis, "The Arctic Ocean: Promise and Peril," in *Sea Power: The History and Geopolitics of the World's Oceans* (New York: Penguin, 2017), 233–68.

Chapter 15. *Blue Latitudes: Boldly Going Where Captain Cook Has Gone Before*
1. Tony Horwitz, *Blue Latitudes: Boldly Going Where Captain Cook Has Gone Before* (New York: Henry Holt, 2002), 4.

Chapter 16. *Captain Cook: Master of the Seas*
1. Frank McLynn, *Captain Cook: Master of the Seas* (New Haven, Conn.: Yale University Press, 2011), 41.
2. McLynn, 1.
3. McLynn, 301.
4. McLynn, 301.
5. McLynn, 17.

Chapter 17. *Kon-Tiki: Six Men Cross the Pacific on a Raft*
1. Thor Heyerdahl, *Kon-Tiki: Six Men Cross the Pacific on a Raft* (New York: Rand-McNally, 1950), 188.
2. Heyerdahl, 297.
3. Heyerdahl, 296.
4. Heyerdahl, 117.

Chapter 18. *Sailing Alone around the World*

1. Joshua Slocum, *Sailing Alone around the World* (Annapolis, Md.: Naval Institute Press, 1985), 64.
2. Slocum, 22.

Chapter 19. *The Conquest of the Ocean: An Illustrated History of Seafaring*

1. Brian Lavery, *The Conquest of the Ocean: An Illustrated History of Seafaring* (London: Dorling Kindersley, 2013), 8.

Chapter 20. *The Endurance: Shackleton's Legendary Antarctic Expedition*

1. Quoted in Caroline Alexander, *The Endurance: Shackleton's Legendary Antarctic Expedition* (New York: Knopf, 1998), 103.
2. Alexander, 152.

Chapter 21. *The Silent World: A Story of Undersea Discovery and Adventure, by the First Men to Swim at Record Depths with the Freedom of Fish*

1. Jacques Cousteau with Frédéric Dumas, *The Silent World: A Story of Undersea Discovery and Adventure by the First Men to Swim at Record Depths with Freedom of Fish* (New York: Harper and Brothers, 1953).
2. Cousteau, 131.
3. Cousteau, 31.
4. Cousteau, 31.
5. Cousteau, 48.

Chapter 22. *20,000 Leagues under the Sea*

1. Jules Verne, *20,000 Leagues under the Sea* (1872; repr., New York: Heritage, 1952), ix. First published in French, *Vingt mille lieues sous les mers: Tour du monde sous-marin* (1871).
2. Verne, *20,000 Leagues*, 149.

Chapter 23. *Master and Commander*

1. Patrick O'Brian, *Master and Commander* (New York: Norton, 1969), 28.

Chapter 24. *Mister Roberts*

1. Thomas Heggen, *Mister Roberts* (Annapolis, Md.: Naval Institute Press, 1992), 9.
2. Heggen, 6.

Chapter 25. *Moby-Dick or, the Whale*

1. Herman Melville, *Moby-Dick or, the Whale* (New York: Harper & Brothers, 1851), 452.
2. New Bedford Whaling Museum, https://www.whalingmuseum.org.

Chapter 26. *Moods of the Sea: Masterworks of Sea Poetry*

1. Thomas Hardy, "The Convergence of the Twain: Lines on the Loss of the *Titanic*," in *Moods of the Sea: Masterworks of Sea Poetry* (Annapolis, Md.: Naval Institute Press, 1981), 119.
2. Alfred, Lord Tennyson, "Ulysses," in *Moods of the Sea: Masterworks of Sea Poetry* (Annapolis, Md.: Naval Institute Press, 1981), 223.
3. Tennyson, "Ulysses," 222.

Chapter 27. *Mutiny on the Bounty*

1. Charles Nordhoff and James Norman Hall, *Mutiny on the Bounty* (Boston: Little, Brown, 1932), 57.

Chapter 28. *Run Silent, Run Deep*

1. Edward L. Beach, *Salt and Steel: Reflections of a Submariner* (Annapolis, Md.: Naval Institute Press, 1999), 289.
2. Edward L. Beach, *Run Silent, Run Deep* (New York: Henry Holt, 1955; repr., Annapolis, Md.: Naval Institute Press, 1983).

Chapter 29. *Short Stories of the Sea*

1. George C. Solley and Eric Steinbaugh, eds., *Short Stories of the Sea*, with introduction and biographies by David O. Tomlinson (Annapolis, Md.: Naval Institute Press, 1984).

Chapter 30. *The Bedford Incident*

1. Mark Rascovich, *The Bedford Incident* (New York: Atheneum, 1963), 307.
2. Rascovich, 337.

Chapter 31. *The Caine Mutiny*

1. Herman Wouk, *The Caine Mutiny: A Novel of World War II* (Garden City, N.Y.: Doubleday, 1951), 354.
2. In 1842 mutineers plotted a potential uprising in the U.S. Navy Brig USS *Somers*, but it was detected and stopped before it came to fruition.

Chapter 32. *The Cruel Sea*

1. Nicholas Monsarrat, *The Cruel Sea*, as quoted in James Stavridis and Robert Girrier, *Command at Sea* (Annapolis, Md.: Naval Institute Press, 2010), 1.
2. James Stavridis, "What Was Life Like for Sailors in the Battle of the Atlantic," *New York Times Magazine*, April 14, 2020, https://www.nytimes.com/2020/04/14/magazine/world-war-ii-battle-of-atlantic-sailors.html.

Chapter 33. *The Good Shepherd*
1. C. S. Forester, *The Good Shepherd* (Boston: Little, Brown, 1955), 158.
2. Forester, 3.

Chapter 34. *Life of Pi*
1. Yann Martel, *Life of Pi* (New York: Harcourt, 2001), 97.
2. Martel, 162.
3. Martel, 225.

Chapter 35. *The Old Man and the Sea*
1. Ernest Hemingway, *The Old Man and the Sea* (New York: Scribner, 1952), 104.
2. Hemingway, 83.
3. Hemingway, 114.

Chapter 36. *Turner & the Sea*
1. Christine Riding and Richard Johns, *Turner and the Sea* (London: Thames & Hudson, 2013), 23.

Chapter 37. *The Autobiography of George Dewey: Admiral of the United States Navy and Hero of the Spanish-American War*
1. George Dewey, *The Autobiography of George Dewey* (Annapolis, Md.: Naval Institute Press, 1987), v.
2. Dewey, 132.
3. Dewey, 61–95.
4. Eric Smith, Introduction to *The Autobiography of George Dewey* (Annapolis, Md.: U.S. Naval Institute Press Classics of Naval Literature, 1987), xi.

Chapter 38. *Empires of the Sea: The Siege of Malta, the Battle of Lepanto, and the Contest for the Center of the World*
1. Roger Crowley, *Empires of the Sea: The Siege of Malta, the Battle of Lepanto, and the Contest for the Center of the World* (New York: Random House, 2008), 276.
2. Crowley, xv.

Chapter 39. *In the Heart of the Sea: The Tragedy of the Whaleship* Essex
1. Herman Melville, *Moby-Dick or, the Whale* (New York: Harper & Brothers, 1851).
2. Tim Severin, *In Search of Moby Dick: The Quest for the White Whale* (New York: Basic Books, 2000).

Chapter 40. *Lady in the Navy: A Personal Reminiscence*
1. Joy Bright Hancock, *Lady in the Navy: A Personal Reminiscence* (Annapolis, Md.: Naval Institute Press, 1972), 266.

2. Hancock, 37.
3. Hancock, 40.
4. Hancock, 41.
5. Naval History and Heritage Command, biography of Joy Bright Hancock, https:// www.history.navy.mil/content/history/nhhc/research/histories/biographies-list/bios-h /hancock-joy-bright.html.

Chapter 41. *One Hundred Days: The Memoirs of the Falklands Battle Group Commander*
1. Margaret Thatcher, Forward to *One Hundred Days: The Memoirs of the Falklands Battle Group Commander*, by Adm. Sandy Woodward with Patrick Robinson (Annapolis, Md.: Naval Institute Press, 1992), xiii.
2. Thatcher, xii–xiii
3. Woodward, *One Hundred Days*, 146.
4. Woodward, 114.
5. Woodward, 334.

Chapter 42. *Sea of Thunder: Four Commanders and the Last Great Naval Campaign, 1941–1945*
1. Evan Thomas, *Sea of Thunder: Four Commanders and the Last Great Naval Campaign 1941–1945* (New York: Simon & Schuster, 2006), 300.
2. Thomas, 349.
3. Thomas, 339.
4. Thomas, 353.
5. Thomas, 291.

Chapter 43. *She Captains: Heroines and Hellions of the Sea*
1. Joan Druett, *She Captains: Heroines and Hellions of the Sea* (New York: Simon & Schuster, 2000), 96.
2. Druett, 35.
3. Druett, 54.
4. Druett, 266.

Chapter 44. *The Battle of Salamis: The Naval Encounter That Saved Greece—and Western Civilization*
1. About the battle itself, see James Stavridis, *Sea Power: The History and Geopolitics of the World's Oceans* (New York: Penguin Press, 2017); and about the Greek admiral Themistocles, see James Stavridis, *Sailing True North: Ten Admirals and the Voyage of Character* (New York: Penguin Press, 2019).
2. Barry Strauss, *The Battle of Salamis: The Naval Encounter That Saved Greece—and Western Civilization* (New York: Simon & Schuster, 2004).

3. Strauss, 7.

4. Quoted in Strauss, 202.

Chapter 45. *The Influence of Seapower upon History, 1660–1783*

1. Portions of this short essay are drawn from Admiral James Stavridis, *Sailing True North: Ten Admirals and the Voyage of Character* (New York: Penguin, 2019).

2. James Stavridis and Robert Girrier, *Division Officer's Guide*, 12th ed. (Annapolis, Md.: Naval Institute Press, 2017); James Stavridis, Robert Girrier, Tom Ogden, and Jeff Heames, *Watch Officer's Guide*, 16th ed. (Annapolis, Md.: Naval Institute Press, 2020); James Stavridis and Robert Girrier, *Command at Sea*, 6th ed. (Annapolis, Md.: Naval Institute Press, 2010); James Stavridis, *Destroyer Captain: Lessons of a First Command* (Annapolis, Md.: Naval Institute Press, 2008); James Stavridis, *The Accidental Admiral: A Sailor Takes Command at NATO* (Annapolis, Md.: Naval Institute Press, 2014); James Stavridis and R. Manning Ancell, *The Leader's Bookshelf* (Annapolis, Md.: Naval Institute Press, 2017); and now, of course, *The Sailor's Bookshelf.*

3. Alfred Thayer Mahan, *The Influence of Sea Power upon History, 1660–1783* (1890; repr. New York: Hill & Wang, 1957).

Chapter 46. *The Navy as a Fighting Machine*

1. Bradley Fiske, *The Navy as a Fighting Machine* (1916; repr., Annapolis: U.S. Naval Institute Press, 1988), xiii.

2. James Stavridis, *Sailing True North: Ten Admirals and the Voyage of Character* (New York: Penguin, 2019).

3. Clark G. Reynolds, *Famous American Admirals* (Annapolis, Md.: Naval Institute Press, 2002), 118.

4. John B. Hattendorf, B. Mitchell Simpson, and John R. Wadleigh, *Sailors and Scholars: The Centennial History of the U.S. Naval War College* (Newport, R.I.: U.S. Naval War College Press, 1984), 85.

5. Fiske, *The Navy as a Fighting Machine*, 57.

6. Reynolds, *Famous American Admirals*, 119.

7. Paolo E. Coletta, *Admiral Bradley A. Fiske and the American Navy* (Lawrence: Regents of the University of Kansas Press, 1979), 225.

Chapter 47. *The Perfect Storm: A True Story of Men against the Sea*

1. Quoted in Sebastian Junger, *The Perfect Storm: A True Story of Men against the Sea* (New York: Norton, 1997), 5.

2. Junger, 78.

3. Junger, 54.

4. Junger, 102.

Chapter 48. *The Seafarers.* Time-Life twenty-two-volume series, 1978–81
1. *The Seafarers,* 22 volumes (New York: Time-Life Books, 1978–81).

Chapter 49. *Trailblazer: The U.S. Navy's First Black Admiral*
1. Samuel Gravely, *Trailblazer: The U.S. Navy's First Black Admiral* (Annapolis, Md.: Naval Institute Press, 2010), 93.
2. Gravely, 179.
3. Gravely, 96.
4. Gravely, 222.
5. Alma Gravely, Afterword to Gravely, *Trailblazer,* 253.
6. Gravely, 262.

Chapter 50. *Two Years before the Mast: A Personal Narrative of Life at Sea*
1. Richard Henry Dana Jr., *Two Years before the Mast: A Personal Narrative of Life at Sea,* ed. by Thomas Philbrick (New York: Penguin, 1981), 462–63.
2. Dana, 125.
3. Dana, 42.
4. Richard Henry Dana Jr., *Two Years before the Mast: A Personal Narrative of Life at Sea* (Norwalk, Conn.: Heritage Press, 1947), 292.

Conclusion
1. Robert Kaplan, *Asia's Cauldron: The South China Sea and the End of a Stable Pacific* (New York: Random House, 2014).
2. Jean-Yves Delitte and Giuseppe Baiguera, *Great Naval Battles of the Twentieth Century* (Annapolis, Md.: Naval Institute Press, 2020).
3. James Stavridis, *Sea Power: The History and Geopolitics of the World's Ocean* (New York: Penguin, 2017).
4. Eugene O'Neill, *Seven Plays of the Sea* (New York: Vintage, 1972).
5. John Steele Gordon, *A Thread across the Ocean: The Heroic Story of the Transatlantic Cable* (New York: Walker, 2002).
6. Hampton Sides, *Into the Kingdom of Ice: The Grand and Terrible Polar Voyage of USS Jeannette* (New York: Knopf Doubleday, 2014).
7. Laurence Bergreen, *Over the Edge of the World: Magellan's Terrifying Circumnavigation of the Globe* (New York: Harper Perennial, 2004).
8. Walter R. Borneman, *The Admirals: Nimitz, Halsey, Leahy, and King—The Five-Star Admirals Who Won the War at Sea* (New York: Little, Brown, 2012).
9. Craig L. Symonds, *Decision at Sea: Five Naval Battles That Shaped History* (Oxford: Oxford University Press, 2005).
10. Ian McGuire, *The North Water: A Novel* (New York: Henry Holt, 2016).

11. Herman Melville, *Billy Budd, Sailor* (1924; repr., Chicago: University of Chicago Press, 1962).

12. Marcus Goodrich, *Delilah* (1941; repr., Annapolis, Md.: Naval Institute Press, 1985).

13. Samuel Eliot Morison, *The Two-Ocean War: A Short History of the United States Navy* (1963; repr., Annapolis, Md.: Naval Institute Press, 2007).

14. James D. Hornfischer, *The Last Stand of the Tin Can Sailors: The Extraordinary World War II Story of the U.S. Navy's Finest Hour* (New York: Random House, 2004).

15. J. H. Parry, *Trade and Dominion: The European Overseas Empires in the Eighteenth Century* (London: Weidenfeld and Nicolson, 1971).

16. Samuel Taylor Coleridge, *The Rime of the Ancient Mariner*, ed. by Paul H. Fry (Boston: Bedford/St. Martin's, 1999).

ABOUT THE
AUTHOR

A 1976 distinguished graduate of the U.S. Naval Academy, **Adm. James Stavridis** spent more than thirty-five years on active service in the U.S. Navy. He commanded destroyers and a carrier strike group in combat and served for seven years as a four-star admiral, culminating with four years as the sixteenth Supreme Allied Commander at NATO. He holds a PhD in international relations and is Dean of the Fletcher School of Law and Diplomacy at Tufts University. Admiral Stavridis has written ten books and hundreds of articles on global security issues and leadership.